A Wake Up Call for Your Golf Game

The Ultimate Improvement Guide

by John Randle
Canadian PGA

Printed in Victoria, Canada

National Library of Canada Cataloguing in Publication

Randle, John S. (John Stevenson), 1966-
    A wake up call for your golf game / John S. Randle.
ISBN 1-55395-778-4
    1. Golf. I. Title.
GV965.R33 2003   796.352'3   C2003-900761-8

This book was published *on-demand* in cooperation with Trafford Publishing.
On-demand publishing is a unique process and service of making a book available for retail sale to the public taking advantage of on-demand manufacturing and Internet marketing. **On-demand publishing** includes promotions, retail sales, manufacturing, order fulfilment, accounting and collecting royalties on behalf of the author.

Suite 6E, 2333 Government St., Victoria, B.C. V8T 4P4, CANADA

Phone	250-383-6864	Toll-free	1-888-232-4444 (Canada & US)
Fax	250-383-6804	E-mail	sales@trafford.com
Web site	www.trafford.com	TRAFFORD PUBLISHING IS A DIVISION OF TRAFFORD HOLDINGS LTD.	
Trafford Catalogue #03-0141	www.trafford.com/robots/03-0141.html		

10   9   8   7   6   5   4

About the Author

John Randle has been around golf his entire life. His father got him started in golf at age 11 and John continues to be active in what he calls, "the greatest game on earth".

His competitive background includes junior golf at a national level and U.S. College Golf at the University of Washington where he earned a Bachelors Degree in Psychology. After university, John turned pro and played "on tour" for seven years. His travels included two years on the South African Tour, seven years as a full time member of the Canadian Tour (he is still a veteran member) and were hilighted by two events on the PGA Tour. His playing accomplishments include over 40 professional tournament wins including the prestigious British Columbia PGA Championship. John has held five course records and continues to play a full tournament schedule.

For the past six years John has focused his efforts on helping others learn the great game of golf. A testament to his dedication to developing his teaching skills is his being awarded the BC PGA Teacher of the Year award in 2002.

He has written over 50 instructional articles for several publications and is quickly becoming one of Canada's most respected teachers. His life-long quest for golfing excellence coupled with his passion for teaching has led to this, his first instructional book.

John has faith in every golfer's ability to improve. He feels the reason most golfers struggle to improve, is that the information they are using is incorrect.

John has lived in Victoria, BC, Canada most of his life. He is a Canadian PGA Teaching Professional at the GBC Golf Academy at Olympic View Golf Course in Victoria, BC.

acknowledgements

As I sit here about to write my first instructional book, I find myself reflecting on all the people and events that have helped me reach this point in my career. To my parents, for introducing me to the greatest game on earth and providing me with unconditional support and opportunity, I am eternally grateful. To my lovely wife, Lori, who is also a teaching professional, thank you for your unwavering belief in me, your continuing support and all the lessons you have taught me about life and golf. To my many friends in the golf business who have helped shape my ideas about the game and the best ways to help people learn it, I couldn't have written this book without you. To my thousands of students, who have taught me so much about the game and my teaching abilities, thank you for entrusting me with your golf games.

I have spent the last twenty-five years playing the great game of golf and the last six or seven teaching the game. Over these many years I have taken many lessons, given many lessons, read hundreds of books and magazine articles, and had uncountable discussions about the game with fellow professionals. These experiences have shaped who I am and what I know and believe with regards to the game of golf. The ideas and concepts you will read on the coming pages are what I believe to be true. They represent my philosophy of the best way to approach the learning of the game of golf.

I willingly acknowledge that many of my ideas about the game of golf were pioneered by other professionals. Like most teachers, I have taken bits and pieces from many sources and combined them with my own beliefs to form the viewpoint that will be reflected in this book.

Finally, to everyone involved with the production of <u>A Wake Up Call for Your Golf Game</u>, I literally couldn't have done it without you. To Olympic View Golf Course, which I now call home, thank you for the use of your wonderful practice facility where all of the pictures were taken. To Werner and Regula Strickler from Photo Srickler, thank you for your patience and professionalism. To Wayne Carlson, the artist responsible for all the great drawings, I hope your golfing skills will someday be close to your artistic abilities. You will certainly be on tour if that is the case. Last but not least, to all the folks at Trafford Publishing in Victoria, I know you have hundreds of clients but you always made me feel like I was the only one.

Once again, thanks to everyone who has helped me reach this point. I hope you all understand what a big part you have played in my life thus far, and that you will continue to be a part of my life in the future.

introduction

Much is written about the advanced technology that goes into golf clubs, and golf courses are in better condition than ever before. Why then, is the golfing population at almost the same skill level as it was 20 years ago? If the clubs are getting better and the courses are getting better, it must be us. Specifically, it must be the way we approach the game.

I wrote this book with one goal in mind, to make golfers aware of the steps needed to improve their games. I believe these steps are:

- Fully understand the key concepts, which govern the various techniques in golf.
- Use these concepts to develop the best technique possible given your physical capabilities and goals.
- Utilize proper practice methods to strengthen these techniques and create solid habits while spending appropriate time on every part of the game.
- Develop the mental skills required to allow your physical capabilities to be reached on a regular basis.
- Learn to make good strategy decisions on the course that are consistent with your present ability level.
- Get out of your own way and just play golf; become engrossed with the process of sending the golf ball to the target.

I began playing golf when I was ten years old. When I was about fourteen, I decided I would play professional golf when I grew up. I progressed through the junior ranks, played college golf at the University of Washington and played "on tour" for seven years before turning my focus to helping others improve their golf games. In short, I have spent a large portion of my life (20 years) trying to improve my own golf game and the last six years, devoted to helping others.

When I first began teaching golf, I couldn't understand why my students didn't seem to show much improvement, even after what I thought were really good lessons. As time wore on and my teaching skills became more polished, I began to see more improvement in my students but they were still falling well short of their potential. After many more lessons and continued reflection on the situation, I feel I have come to terms with the primary reasons golfers generally don't improve. In fact, I now understand why I didn't have a more successful playing career. My swing and short game were really quite sound but I was making the same mistakes that keep most golfers from ever really improving.

This book will provide you with guidance on how to play better golf. It is my goal to help you avoid the classic errors almost every golfer makes in his or her approach to improvement. If you truly want to better your golf game, you will use the information from this book and combine it with some professional golf instruction from a qualified PGA Teaching Professional in your area. I will offer some instruction similar to conventional instructional books on topics like how to hold the club, where to position the golf ball and so on, but these areas are better learned with the help of personalized lessons. The most important parts of this book will focus on three vital areas for your improvement:

1. The three concepts most golfers misunderstand about the golf swing that need to be clearly understood in order to build a consistent golf swing.

2. There are many parts of the game and you need to practice all of them to shoot lower scores and have more fun on the course.

3. Good practice skills are needed to build a total golf game that will let you play your best golf all the time, even when the pressure is on.

Please remember, as you read this book and realize you may have been making some mistakes in your approach to golf improvement, these are the same mistakes I was making and I was a Tour Pro! You will also notice my ideas suggest you practice differently than how you see other golfers, even good golfers, practice. It is widely believed, to be successful, you should observe the masses and do the opposite. In golf, this is definitely true.

I respect you for caring enough about your golf game to buy this book. I know the information you are soon to read will help you become a much better golfer and you will have much more fun playing the best game on earth.

How to Use This Book

This handbook will provide golfers with the information needed to learn the game. There are sections on equipment, the full swing, putting, the scoring game, the mental game, course management and specialty shots. Each section offers information on the various skills required and advice on the best ways to practice. You will also find a complete section on how to learn the game, starting on page 143, so you can really streamline your improvement and achieve the quickest results possible.

The entire book has been written assuming the reader is a right-handed swinger of the club. Whenever possible, I have used general terms in my descriptions but there are times when I needed to be more specific. In certain situations, it is much more clear to use right and left, rather than trying to use words like front and back. Being Canadian, I know about 1 in every 5 golfers from Canada swings left-handed, although, the percentage in the rest of the world is only about 5%. Do you think that has anything to do with hockey? If you are left-handed, please accept my apologies. I know lefties have been getting the short end of the golfing stick for many years and it certainly isn't my desire to add to your torment. I hope you can switch the directions to fit your needs. I honestly believe less people will be confused this way but I do feel badly that the oppressed minority known as "South Paws" are being mistreated, yet again.

In the text of the book, you will come across words, which are in *bold and italic print*. If you are unfamiliar with these words, their definitions are in the glossary starting on page 169. It would be a good idea for you to read the glossary first to familiarize yourself with many of the golf related words that appear in this book.

In the Appendices at the back of the book, you will find five resources designed to aid you in your quest for a better golf game.

Appendix A - "A Total Game Checklist"

This is a checklist of the main concepts and skills needed for you to reach your golfing potential.

Appendix B - Putting Assessment Form

This is a simple test you can use to assess your putting game, allocate practice time and chart your improvement over time.

Appendix C - Scoring Game Assessment Form

This is a simple test for your scoring shots to assess your scoring game, allocate practice time and chart your improvement.

Appendix D - Game Statistics Form

This is a great form for keeping track of how you arrive at your scores each day.

Appendix E - Goal Setting Forms

Goals provide the road map for success and these forms will help you organize yours.

This book is not intended to give you all the instruction you will ever need to become a great golfer. I feel it is very difficult to learn physical skills by reading a book. I wrote this book to shine a light on the need to practice every part of the game, the three vital concepts that form the foundation for building a swing and effective practice methods needed to make permanent improvements to your entire game. I believe these elements, when combined with professional instruction, will be a recipe for reaching your golfing goals.

I urge you to take the information in this book to heart and also find a teaching pro to whom you can relate, for personalized help with your entire game.

Good luck and enjoy the journey!

Table of Contents

Section Three - *Learning and Improving*

Section One

A Foundation of Knowledge

Chapter One
Why Most Golfers Don't Improve

There are a few reasons why most golfers don't improve their golf games. The most prevalent is simply that most golfers don't practice. If you are too busy or golf is not a high priority in your life, I completely understand, but to improve at golf, you need both the desire and the time to invest in your skills.

This book is for golfers who are interested in taking the necessary steps to improve, and will provide a guide for total game improvement. By total game improvement, I mean raising your skill level in all of the different facets of golf so you can shoot lower scores. The ultimate goal in golf is to shoot the lowest score possible. This book is written with this philosophy in mind. If your goals are different, maybe something more specific, like hitting the ball more consistently, this book will also provide you with instruction tailored to each phase of the game.

I believe there are three major reasons most golfers fail to improve:

1. Most golfers misunderstand the three main concepts of the golf swing that govern how the club should be used through impact. Working with the correct information is absolutely critical for building a repeating swing.

2. Most golfers spend 95% of their available practice time on the full swing, which represents a much smaller percentage of the game. This approach makes it impossible to achieve your lowest possible scores.

3. Most golfers have poor practice skills. The typical golfer fails to understand the difference between technique practice and golf practice. As a result, most golfers struggle to improve their swings and never really learn the skills needed to play well on the course.

The golfing establishment is partly responsible for the way golfers approach the game. Most teaching professionals say they offer golf lessons but the majority only give "golf swing lessons". As I will point out in Chapter Four, the golf swing is only one of many parts to the game and should, therefore, be one of many topics covered by instruction. If golf professionals are focusing too heavily on the swing, how is the average golfer to know any different?

Most golfers also approach game improvement hap-hazardly without any kind of structured plan. This lack of goal setting often leads to inefficient practice and adds considerable time to the improvment process if not sabotaging the golfer's efforts all together.

Even when golfers do make good decisions and are working to make positive changes to their games, the vast majority gives up on the changes before they have a chance to take hold. New habits or skills take time to integrate into your game, so patience is very necessary as you attempt to improve.

Study All the Subjects

If you go to a driving range that has hitting stalls and an area for practicing the short game you will see a perfect example of why golfers fail to improve. Almost everyone there will be rapidly pounding golf balls into the driving range and few, if any golfers, will be honing their scoring skills. I will break the game down for you in Chapter Three but for now I will leave with an analogy.

Just like in school, to "pass" as a golfer you will need to study EVERY subject.

Imagine when you were back in school that you spent nearly all of your study time on your math skills. You would have ended up being a math whiz but since your advancement to the next grade was dependent on your performance in all subjects, you would wind up having to repeat the same grade over and over again. Golf is the same. To become a better golfer and move up to the next "grade", you will have to study all the subjects.

Use the Correct Information

I have taught many athletes who have been able to reach a very high level in other sports but really struggle with learning the golf swing. The reason isn't that they have lost their athleticism or that the golf swing is much more difficult to learn than other sports. They struggle because the information they are using when trying to learn the swing is incorrect and eliminates their chance to be successful.

It has been my experience most golfers misunderstand one or more of the three major concepts, which govern how the club should swing through the ball. Understanding how to make solid contact, control the clubface and swing the club on the correct path are at the root of learning a repeating swing.

Every good golf swing satisfies the conditions above. In fact, the quality of a golf swing should be judged solely on its ability to deliver the club to the back of the ball correctly and consistently. If you look at all the players on the pro tours, the way their golf clubs perform as they swing through impact are all very similar. The physics of how the club needs to be swung into the golf ball to create a straight golf shot is the same no matter who you are, or how you are built. There is an old saying that the golf ball "doesn't know your name", it only knows what your club tells it. This is the reason that golfers of all sizes and strengths, with different looking swings, can all learn to hit the ball straight.

Once a golfer learns WHAT the club needs to do as it swings through the ball, he or she can begin the process of learning HOW his or her body needs to perform to make it happen, with consideration given to body type, flexibility and injuries.

Most golfers struggle because they misunderstand the major concepts and are trying to build a swing based on completely wrong assumptions. Stay tuned for a detailed description of each concept in Chapter Two to find out if you are using the correct information.

Practice Effectively

The final reason most golfers don't improve is that the quality of their practice is very poor. In addition to spending far too much time practicing only the golf swing, neglecting other parts of the game, most golfers spend their time working on the golf swing ineffectively. In Section Three of the book, I detail the steps to ensuring your practice time is most effective.

Topics to be covered in Section Three include: deciding what to practice, how to practice and the role of a qualified teaching professional in your improvement program.

It is my sincere hope that after reading the rest of my book, you will have all the information needed to reach your golfing goals. I think golf is the best game on earth and I see so many avid golfers who are frustrated with their games. Golf should be fun and I think if you take the following chapters to heart and apply the ideas to your game, you will definitely improve and begin having more fun on the course.

Chapter Summary

There are three main reasons for not improving:

- using the wrong information while building your swing

- not practicing all parts of the game

- ineffective practice habits

Chapter Two
Three Concepts Vital to a Consistent Swing

To build and maintain a consistent golf swing, you must first understand the concepts that govern how the club needs to be used during the forward swing. To hit good golf shots, the golf club must make solid contact with the ball, the clubface must return to a *square* position as it strikes the ball, and the club needs to be swinging towards the target as it passes through the impact zone. Learning these skills is only possible by using the proper swing concepts and combining them with your physical capabilities to develop YOUR best swing.

Most golfers understand the need for solid contact, a square clubface and proper swing path, but many haven't had these concepts explained to them correctly. They are stuck using wrong information as they attempt to learn a swing.

Here are three common misconceptions that make learning a swing very difficult:

1. Many golfers wrongly think that, to get the ball in the air, they must help it into the air by lifting it with their swings. The result is inconsistent contact.

2. Many golfers misunderstand how to control the clubface to create straight shots, and end up struggling with a *slice*.

3. Many golfers, because they chronically slice the ball, feel the correct path is considerably to the left of ideal.

All Sizes and Shapes

You have probably noticed there isn't a set body type needed to play good golf. While having a tall and lean body is probably an advantage, a la Tiger Woods, there are plenty of world-class players who have distinctly different body types; Craig Stadler and Ian Woosnam spring to mind. What these and all great players have in common is their ability to make a swing that delivers the club to the back of the ball as is necessary for a good golf shot. To build a repeating swing, you must first understand how the club needs to be used and then learn how your body needs to move to make it happen.

Three Important Concepts

To hit a straight golf shot, the golf club must approach the ball from *inside* the target line and swing out, towards the target as the clubface is squaring to the target. This will result in a club that is travelling down the target line and a clubface that is facing the target at impact. When you combine these factors with solid contact, you will hit a good golf shot. Many golfers already know these theories but many don't. By the end of this chapter, you will have a clear understanding of all these concepts and you can use this knowledge as a foundation for your golf swing.

Getting Solid Contact

Solid contact can be defined as the contacting of the middle of the golf ball with the middle of the clubface. This is a learned skill that relies on four things. These are: understanding how the club needs to swing to create solid contact, proper ball position in your stance, relatively sound technique, and practice time spent learning the skill. I will discuss the technique and practice portions of the equation later in the book. Let's begin by understanding the ideal motion of the club and how ball position affects the ability to achieve solid contact.

Many golfers struggle with making solid contact because they think they need to help lift the ball into the air with their swings. They often describe this effort as trying to "get under the ball". This thought process can cause you to drop your rear shoulder and hang back on your rear foot in an attempt to get the club to approach the ball from underneath. This leads to the bottom of your swing arc happening behind the ball. If the club strikes the ground you will hit a *fat shot* and if the club misses the ground before the ball, you will generally hit a topped shot or miss the ball entirely because the club is on its way back up when it gets to the ball. When people hit behind the ball, they often say "I dropped my shoulder", and when they top the ball a typical response is, "I lifted my head".

> *Trying to "get under" the ball will often cause you to drop your rear shoulder and either hit behind or top the ball.*

These statements may be true, but the ultimate cause of these destructive behaviors is an attempt to swing the club up into the ball.

When the ball is on a tee or in longer grass, swinging up into the ball can work because there is actually air under the ball. Unfortunately, when the ball is sitting on firmer ground, or worse yet, in a divot, there isn't any air under the ball, so swinging up is impossible. This is why most beginner golfers prefer the ball to be on a high tee, or in the rough, where there is air under the ball. Conversely, most advanced players prefer the ball on a lower tee or tightly cut fairway where they have more control over the shot.

To achieve solid contact on shots played off the ground, you must understand that the club needs to swing down through the ball making contact with the ground just after impact. In other words, the bottom of your swing arc must be located after the ball, resulting in a divot or small scuffmark being made after the ball has been struck.

If you watch the professionals on TV hit iron shots, you will notice they always take divots. The key point to understand is they are taking the divot after the ball is gone. They take these divots, rather than picking the ball right off the top of the turf, because it makes hitting the ball off firm ground or short grass easier. Secondly, swinging the club down through the ball and taking a divot after impact, gives them a larger margin for error.

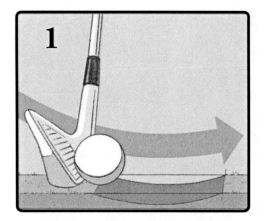
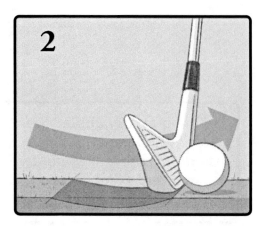

Consistently solid contact on iron shots is achieved with a descending blow as in Picture 1, not by trying to lift the ball as in Picture 2.

By swinging the club down through the ball, all you have to accomplish to get the ball in the air is have the *leading edge* contact the ball below the equator while on its way down into the ground. If this occurs, the ball will roll up the face of the iron and get into the air. In short, by swinging the club down through the ball and taking a divot, you have the benefit of almost ¾ of an inch (half the ball) of leeway to get decent results. Perfectly solid contact will happen when the middle of the clubface contacts the ball but as long as you are close, and using the technique described above, you will get consistent results.

Good contact is promoted by correctly placing the ball in your stance. Ideally, the bottom of your swing arc will happen when your lead arm and shaft reach a vertical position in the forward swing. This happens roughly opposite the instep of your front foot. Your more lofted clubs are built to work best when the ball is positioned in the middle of your stance, well before the bottom of the swing. As the clubs get longer and have less loft, they are built to work better when striking the ball closer to the bottom of your swing.

The ideal divot is not more than a half inch deep. Your club should remove the roots of the grass but not much of the soil. If your divots are more than a half inch in depth, it indicates your golf club is approaching the ball on too steep an angle.

For these reasons, a general guideline for proper ball position is near the middle of your stance for your wedges and progressively farther forward as the clubs get longer. When hitting woods off a tee, a level approach of the clubhead to the back of the ball is needed, so the ball should be placed at the bottom of your swing, roughly even with the instep of the front foot. These are only general parameters. Your particular ball position should be based on the actual location of your swing's lowest point.

To summarize, your ability to locate the bottom of your swing correctly and achieve solid contact will be a combination of understanding the concept of solid contact, positioning the ball correctly in your stance, spending time to learn the skill, and having a golf swing which is good enough to let you develop the skill to a level which satisfies your needs.

Ball position varies depending on the club.

Controlling the Clubface

"Controlling the clubface" means having the ability to return the clubface to a square position at impact. This is the most important skill you will need to acquire to play good golf.

Control over the clubface is made possible by these factors:

- ▶ Establishing a good relationship between your hands and the club by forming a fundamentally sound grip on the club.

- ▶ Gaining an understanding of how the club needs to be used.

- ▶ Becoming acutely aware of how your hands and the club relate.

- ▶ Spending sufficient time to learn the timing needed to have the clubface square to the target at impact.

As you will read over the next few pages, controlling the closing of the clubface will rely on your understanding of how the clubface and your hands relate to each other. You will also need to spend sufficient time practicing the movement to learn the timing required to close the clubface at the right time. The good news is, you already have well developed, fine-motor skills, which allow you to accurately control the movement and orientation of your hands. You will use those skills to learn how to control the clubface and hit straight golf shots.

> *To be square at impact the club must swing from*
> *open to closed as it swings through the ball.*

Many golfers slice the golf ball because they try to keep the clubface square to the target through impact. Unfortunately, this mindset causes the clubface to be open at impact. Quite often, a golfer's attempts to keep the clubface from closing will also lead to problems with balance and distance. It is vital for you to understand that the clubface must be in the process of closing as it passes through the ball.

> *Attempting to hold the clubface*
> *square to the target through*
> *impact causes an open*
> *clubface at impact and the*
> *slice that comes with it.*

Most people can get their hands to face something with relative ease. This skill can be transferred to a golf club if you place your hands on the club correctly and understand how the clubface relates to your hands. I focus on how to hold the club in detail in Chapter Six. For now, it is only important for you to understand that a proper hold on the club will result in your palms facing in the same direction as the clubface. With your hands in this position, the clubface is basically "sitting" in the palm of your right hand if you are a right-handed golfer. This is a vital concept most golfers have never had explained to them.

You may never have thought of it in these terms but most golfers think of the clubface as sitting in the hand as it appears in picture 1. The clubface actually sits in your hand as it appears in picture 2. Picture 3 shows how the hands are linked to the clubface by the shaft. Understanding this relationship will allow you to control the clubface by learning to control where your hands are facing through impact.

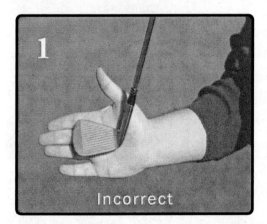
Incorrect

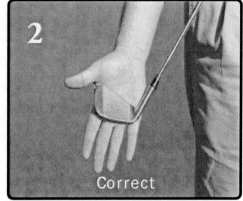
Correct

Understanding how the clubface relates to your hands is critical to your development as a golfer.

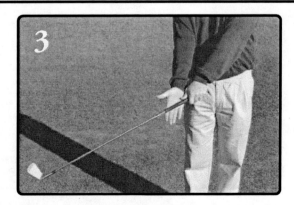

Incorrect Concept and Motion

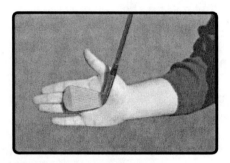

If you incorrectly think the clubface sits in your hand like this ...

... you will think open to close is like this ...

... and you will try to swing like this.

Correct Concept and Motion

If you understand the clubface actually sits in your hand like this ...

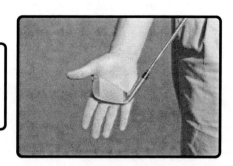

... you will think open to close is like this ...

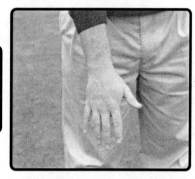

... and you will try to swing like this.

You can see by the photos and descriptons on the previous two pages that your perception of how the clubface relates to your hands will have a huge effect on your ability to deliver the clubface to a square position at impact, and your entire golf swing.

Golfers who hold the club incorrectly, or misinterpret how the clubface relates to their hands, will always struggle to hit the ball straight. Conversely, golfers with good grips and a firm grasp on how the clubface and hands work together, will be able to use the skills they already possess for controlling their hands. With practice, these skills can be quickly transferred to the clubface.

The Correct Swing Path

The proper swing path is the third concept, which must be understood. Many golfers mistakenly think the cause of a slice or *hook* is an improper swing path. In actual fact, a swing path, either to the left or right of the target, is usually a golfer's reaction to the anticipated curvature on his or her shot. Many golfers have distorted ideas about the correct swing path because all of their golf shots curve.

To fix your slice or hook, you must first learn to control the clubface so it returns to a square position at impact. Without curvature on your shots, you are ready to learn to swing the club down the *target line* through impact. Assuming you can learn to consistently square the clubface, the proper path is one where the clubhead approaches the ball from inside the target line (picture 1), and swings out through the ball towards the target (picture 2). For most golfers, this path will feel like it is "inside-to-out" but the correct path is actually "inside to square".

The proper path happens when the clubhead approaches the ball from the inside and swings out towards the target through impact.

I will spend time on how to learn these three, all important, skills in the practice section of the book which begins on page 143. The golf ball will be your ultimate coach because it tells you exactly what your club was doing at impact.

> **tip time!**
>
> *The golf ball is your best coach. Its flight will tell you what your club was doing at impact and help you learn a good swing.*

To understand the feedback your golf ball is providing, you will need to have a firm grasp on the "Ball Flight Laws".

Ball Flight Laws

The ball flight laws describe the various shapes of shots you can hit and what the club does to cause these nine possible shots. The three concepts described earlier in this chapter are solid contact, square clubface and proper swing path. The golf ball will give you feedback needed to learn each of these skills.

Solid Contact

For solid contact, it is important that you get feedback, which tells you where on the face you have just hit the ball. Most beginner and intermediate golfers have trouble discerning the actual impact point on the clubface. To help ensure you are using the correct impact information I suggest you use tape on the face of your club to show you where the ball was struck. There are labels you can buy, which stick to the clubface, or you can use something as simple as duck tape. To learn solid contact, you need to have accurate feedback about the impact you are making.

The other two important considerations are the shot's initial direction and the curvature during the flight of the ball.

Swing Path

The shot's initial direction is determined mostly by the path of the swinging club. The club can either swing to the left of the target line, straight down the target line or to the right of the target line. In some cases, when the clubface is dramatically open or closed, the shot's initial direction will be affected.

Assuming the club is facing in the same direction as it is swinging, the shot's initial direction will give you valuable feedback about your swing path:

- If the shot starts left of your target, the club was swinging on a path to the left of the target at impact.
- If the shot starts towards your target, the club was swinging on a path down the target line at impact.
- If the shot starts right of your target, the club was swinging on a path to the right of the target at impact.

Clubface Orientation

The curvature on a golf shot is caused by the clubface's orientation at impact. The clubface can either be *open* at impact, square at impact or *closed* at impact. The ball will curve in the direction the club is facing.

- If the clubface looks left of the swing path at impact, the ball will curve to the left.
- If the clubface looks in the direction of the swing path, the ball will fly straight.
- If the clubface looks right of the swing path at impact, the ball will curve to the right.

The degree of clubface deviation and the velocity of the ball dictates the amount of curvature on the shot. The faster the ball is travelling, the faster it will be spinning and the more it will curve. This is the prime reason our longer clubs tend to curve more than our shorter clubs.

The combination of the three possible paths and three possible clubface orientations creates nine possible ball flights shown in the diagram on the next page. Understanding how the club causes these different shots is vital for you to learn the targeting skills performed during the forward swing.

tip time!

To the right are the nine possible ball flights for right-handed golfers.

Your swing path determines the initial direction and your clubface causes curvature.

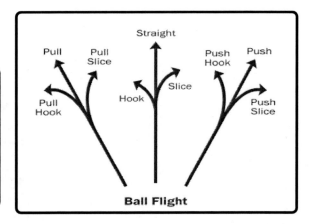

Ball Flight

Chapter Summary

- Iron shots should be struck with a descending blow with the clubhead travelling down and through the ball, making a shallow divot just after impact.

- To be square at impact, the clubface must be closing as it swings through the ball. This closing is learned by understanding how the clubface relates to your hands.

- The proper swing path delivers the clubhead from inside the target line so it is swinging towards the target at impact.

- The golf ball's flight gives you valuable feedback about what the club was doing at impact. This information is vital to learning the golf swing.

One of the most challenging things about learning golf is that many pieces of advice form friends or fellow golfers seem logical but aren't correct.

Chapter Three
Stuff You May Know but Really Need to Forget

It is only fitting that after discussing the key concepts to the development of your swing, I spend some time getting rid of golf's equivalent to old wives' tales. There are a number of widely believed notions about the golf swing, which are perpetuated by well-wishing fellow golfers everywhere. Golf is an activity that, for some reason, makes other golfers feel they can advise you on your golf swing just because they can beat you by two strokes, or they have been playing longer. The following is a selection of popular golf tips that may sound logical, but simply aren't correct, and need to be erased from your golfing database.

"Keep Your Head Still"

Nothing inhibits the body's ability to move naturally more than golfers' attempts to keep their heads perfectly still during the golf swing. This mindset almost always leads to a swing fault referred to as a "reverse pivot" or "reverse weight shift". The picture on the next page shows the effects of trying to keep your head still with my weight moving to my front leg during the backswing. From this position the weight usually returns to the rear leg during the forward swing. Basically, this is the opposite of what you want.

To make a good body turn your head must be free to move laterally during the backswing but should remain at the same height throughout the backswing and into impact. You will find more on the body turn in Chapter Six on the full swing.

Trying to keep your head still often causes a "reverse pivot" and a lot of problems.

"Keep Your Head Down"

Many golfers think the reason they top the ball, or miss it entirely, is they have lifted their heads. It may be true that their heads have lifted during the swing but, in almost every case, the actual cause of the topped shot is the golfer's attempt to swing up during the forward swing, resulting in the bottom of the swing being raised. Understanding the concept of swinging down through the ball to cause solid contact, and spending some practice time to learn this skill will eliminate the topped shot from your reportoire.

I far prefer "keep your eyes on the ball". This will allow you to turn freely during the back-swing and, when the club has made contact with the ball, follow it with your eyes to allow for a full, balanced finish.

"Keep Your Left Arm Straight"

This is another oldie but goodie. The tension created by a golfer's attempts to keep the left arm rigidly straight, often inhibits other, more important movements like wrist hinge and body turn. Let's go with extended, but relaxed, when describing the left arm.

"Bend Your Knees"

Here is another popular piece of advice typically offered shortly after a topped shot. A good set-up position can be ruined by too much knee bend. The knees need to be "unlocked".

The unlocking will center the weight on your feet between your heels and balls, and will put you in balance. Bending your knees a lot will cause your posture to become too erect and will destroy your chances of making a good body turn

Correct

Your knees should be "unlocked" as in picture 1 and not bent a lot as in picture 2.

Incorrect

"Shift Your Weight"

Trying to shift your weight, especially in the backswing, often causes you to slide your hips laterally. Too much hip slide blocks the body's ability to turn effectively and leads to all kinds of problems. The weight shift happens as a result of a proper body turn and not because you physically shift your weight.

Trying to shift your weight can cause you to slide laterally and destroys your swing.

"Turn Your Hips"

This can be good advice in certain situations but for a lot of golfers, trying to turn their hips causes their bodies to turn too quickly and leads to problems. Focus on where the club needs to travel and let the brain figure out exactly when the hips need to turn. If and when you become an advanced player you can become a little pickier about specific parts of your forward swing.

"Thanks But No Thanks"

Depending on your stage of development in golf, you may be subject to well meaning golfers who offer unsolicited advice. It is very important for your game, and your sanity, to be polite but firm with your would-be instructor. Regardless of your skill level I recommend you find one source of good golf information, preferably a qualified PGA Professional in your home town, and stick with it. It can be very confusing if you try to use tips from various sources, especially if the person offering the tips doesn't teach golf for a living.

Chapter Summary

There are many golf tips that make sense but don't work. If you care about your golf game you will ignore tips from people who don't teach golf for a living.

Chapter Four
An Overview of the Game

The game of golf is really quite simple to describe. You take a number of interesting looking sticks and use them to propel a small, dimpled ball into a hole. You do that eighteen times and then add up your score. The fewer shots you needed to play the course, the better you did. What is not as simple to describe is how to best accomplish this goal. To become good at getting the ball into the hole with relative efficiency, a golfer must have equipment suitable for his or her needs. He or she must also develop a number of different skills requiring strength, feel and mental prowess.

The first skill that springs to most golfer's minds is the full swing used to send the ball long distances. This is also the skill most golfers equate to golfing ability. In fact, most golfers find it hard to distinguish between the ability to swing a golf club, and the ability to play golf. As you will find in the chapters to follow, there are actually many parts of the game that need to be addressed to play your best golf. Shots played with a full swing comprise only about half of your total score.

Let's take a brief look at what else is required to shoot lower scores. A detailed look at each part of the game is coming in the next few chapters. Remember, getting the ball in the hole in as few shots as possible, is the main focus of the game. If you are like many golfers who feel lower scores will come naturally when your swing improves, you may find yourself thinking differently after you finish this book.

Your Equipment

Your equipment needs to be in good working order and includes everything you use to send the ball to the target. Most golfers think of their equipment as their clubs. Your golf equipment needs to be suited to your size, strength, and skill level, but there are more pieces of your equipment. Your brain needs to be nourished and run well to make it a valuable tool rather than an obstacle to performance and your body must be flexible and fit, to make optimal performance possible.

Putting

Putting is a game all its own and makes up roughly 40% of your total score. Golfers generally hold the putter differently than their other clubs, the stroke is different and the putter, itself, is unlike any other club. Your ability to putt well will have the biggest impact on your scoring.

The Scoring Game

The scoring game is made up of the shots played onto the green with less than a full swing, and accounts for about 15% of your score. Some of the techniques closely resemble the full swing, but most involve different set-up positions, special swing motions and the development of "feel", so the golfer can control the distance the ball flies and rolls. Within the scoring game are chipping, pitching, the wedge game and sand play.

The Mental Game

If you are like most golfers you don't spend any time working on this department, but the quality of your mental game will affect all other parts of your game. Good mental skills allow your body to perform at top level. Without good mental skills, you will never reach your physical capabilities on the course. If you are a golfer, who performs well during practice, but struggles on the course, you will want to read the chapter on the mental game closely.

Course Management

Most golfers acknowledge strategy as an important part of the game, but generally lack the decision making skills necessary to efficiently navigate their ball around the golf course. The decisions you make on the course must be consistent with your skills, or disaster is right around the corner.

Special Knowledge

Special knowledge is needed to handle the many different situations the ball can drag you into during a normal round of golf. Hitting shots off side-hill lies, out of deep grass, and around or over obstacles, all require changes to our set-up and swing. I will also cover some strategies to deal with playing in poor weather and tournament play.

Chapter Summary

The game of golf is made up of many parts. To play your best, you will need to pay attention to all of them.

- Your Equipment
- Putting
- The Scoring Game
- The Full Swing
- The Mental Game
- Course Management
- Special Knowledge

Section Two

*The Many Parts
of the Game*

Without golf clubs that are suited to your body type and swing motion, you will never reach your potential as a golfer.

Chapter Five
Your Equipment

Your equipment includes everything you use to propel the ball to the target. With this in mind, I consider your equipment to be comprised of your brain, your body and, of course, your golf clubs.

Your Brain

I have devoted an entire section later in the book to getting your brain in shape to perform well. All I would like to mention at this point, are some of the factors that will make it possible for your brain to function at a high level.

Dietary Factors

The first important nutritional fact you need to know is 75% of your brain is made up of water. If you become dehydrated, your brain cannot function at its best. You can lose focus, make poor decisions, and feel fatigued. In addition to water, golfers also lose a lot of electrolytes during a round. Electrolytes are minerals that help your body transmit nerve impulses and maintain muscle function. It is very important for you to keep your body hydrated during practice or play. Drinking plenty of water before your round, and drinks rich in electrolytes, like Powerade, during your round, will maintain your body's levels.

Remember, dehydration is well under way before you feel thirsty, so don't use thirst as your indication to start hydrating. By then it is too late. You should also avoid drinking caffienated drinks and alcohol, as they are both responsible for excessive dehydration. Foods containing aspartame and MSG have been shown to negatively affect brain function.

Certain foods and minerals are reputed to help with specific parts of the brain's functioning:

- Sunflower seeds, cauliflower and broccoli may cool your temper.
- Chicken may assist with concentration.
- Yogurt can calm your nerves.
- Foods high in protein improve over all brain functioning.

The other main dietary concerns that affect your brain's functioning are those that help stave off fatigue. These foods are described briefly in the next section on the body.

Your Body

The area of physical fitness is becoming increasingly popular amongst golfers. The much publicized workout regiments of Tiger Woods, David Duval, Anika Sorenstam, and others, are drawing attention to the fact the golf swing is very much an athletic endeavor. To perform at your best, it is very clear your body needs to be both strong and flexible. I do not pretend to know everything about golf specific exercise programs, as I am just in the beginning stages of taking better care of my body. It's funny how reaching your mid-thirties has a way of making you realize the importance of diet and exercise! It takes a little longer to warm up and I feel tired some days after playing. I intend to have my body in much better condition by the time you read this book.

If you are a golfer who wants to play at your highest possible level, or would simply like to play two days in a row without pain, I strongly suggest you begin a program to become more fit, or rehab your injuries.

Dietary Factors

What you eat will greatly affect your energy levels. Foods release energy at different rates. For example, foods high in sugar release their energy quickly, giving you a short term boost in energy, but a substantial drop in energy levels shortly after. In general, proteins release energy more slowly, and will provide a more long-term source of stamina. Carbohydrates come in different forms that have different release rates, so can be good for long or short term energy creation.

Good foods for short-term energy:

- bananas
- raisons
- bagels
- boxed cereals
- fast release energy bars

Good foods for long-term energy:

- apples
- grapes
- nuts
- granola
- bars with slow release ingredients

You are what you eat.

Nutrition is very important but can be quite involved. Finding a book on the topic or enlisting the counsel of a nutritionist will be very helpful as you look to control the quality of the gas you are feeding your engine.

Exercise and Injury Treatment

With a little searching, you will be able to find a health care specialist in your area with whom to work. Many chiropractors, physical therapists, massage therapists, and personal trainers are now focusing on working with golfers. I am not suggesting you need to become so serious about your golf that you are spending a lot of time in the gym each week, but working with some kind of flexibility and strength program, will improve your golf game and probably your quality of life.

Two specific conditions, which cause many golfers to have problems with their swing motions, are tightness in the neck, shoulders and back, and a lack of flexibility in the hamstrings. Your ability to make a good body turn in the backswing, is dependant on your ability to turn the torso roughly 90 degrees, while looking towards the ball. If you are a right-handed golfer and have trouble turning your chin to a position over your left shoulder when you are standing erect, you will need to improve your range of motion.

Tightness in the hamstrings makes it difficult for you to maintain your posture position throughout the swing, and can cause problems with making consistent contact.

There are many books available now on specific exercise programs for golf. I urge you to get advice from a trained professional before beginning any kind of stretching, or exercise program. A golf fitness program will usually go through steps focusing on flexibility, core stability, strength training and then speed creation.

Below are a few basic stretches to warm up the main muscles used when making a golf swing, and can be done before you practice or play. Do the stretches slowly and smoothly. You should not feel any pain as you do them. If you are serious about improving your game, you will consult a fitness professional in your area, and begin a golf specific fitness program.

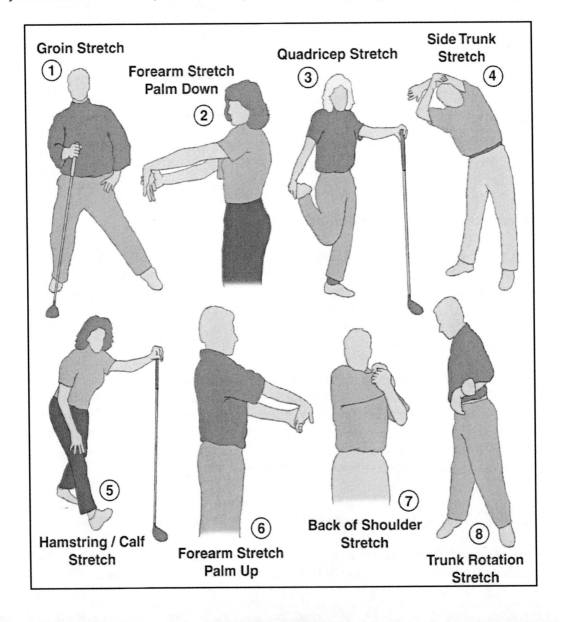

Groin Stretch ①

Forearm Stretch Palm Down ②

Quadricep Stretch ③

Side Trunk Stretch ④

Hamstring / Calf Stretch ⑤

Forearm Stretch Palm Up ⑥

Back of Shoulder Stretch ⑦

Trunk Rotation Stretch ⑧

Your Eyes

Another part of your equipment that will have huge impact on your effectiveness on the course, is your eyes. Your eyes will tell you about slopes and distances, so you need to be able to trust them. Regular eye exams will ensure what you are seeing is actually there!

If you wear sunglasses when you play, be sure to consult an expert, to ensure the lenses are suitable for seeing contrasts, critical for assessing slopes on the greens.

One other note. If you have had progressive lenses prescribed for you, try to use strictly distance glasses for your golf. Progressive lenses often force golfers to bury their chins in their chests to keep the ball in focus, inhibiting the ability to move freely during the swing.

Your Golf Clubs

Your golf clubs need to be carefully selected. Like clothes, they should be the proper size for you. Most people don't go into a store and ask for a pair of pants without making sure they are the correct size and style. Golf clubs need to be selected with the same care. Golfers, from beginners to pros, all need clubs that are suitable for their body types and swings. If you are a beginner, you need to learn with clubs that are right for you, so you won't need to learn a different swing when you finally do get suitable equipment. If you are an experienced player, you need *custom fit* clubs to maximize your talents. You should also take care when deciding which clubs to include in your set.

Set Make-Up

You need a well thought out selection of clubs for your set. Ideally you would start with a perfectly fitted driver, and then add a couple of fairway woods. In addition to the usual 3 or 4-woods, most golfers would be well served by adding 5 and 7-woods to their sets, to replace the 3 and 4-irons. Fairway woods are easier to hit than long irons for most people. The biggest concern when assembling your set is having consitent gaps between the yardages you get with each club. Starting with your wedges, try to have a 10 - 15 yard difference between each club as you go through your set.

Club Specifications

There are many specifications of a golf club, which need to be suitable for your body type and swing, in order for you to perform at your best.

Head Design

You need clubs with the proper weight distribution on the clubhead for your skill level. Most golfers should use clubs that have the majority of the weight located around the perimeter of the head. This, in effect, increases the size of the *sweet spot*, and gives better performance on off-centre hits.

Length

Each club in a set will be a different length, but the entire set needs to be built with your body type and skill in mind. The correct length of your clubs will be determined by your height, the relative length of your arms, and your skill level. You want clubs that are long enough to maximize your club head speed, but not so long that you can't control them.

Lie Angle

Lie angle is the angle at which the shaft comes out of the head. We all make a natural swing with the shaft at a certain angle as it swings through the impact zone. Ideally, the sole of the club will be flat to the ground at impact. For this to happen, the lie angle of the club must be compatible with your swing motion. If the lie angle is incorrect, the toe or heel of the club will be too low at impact, and will cause directional problems.

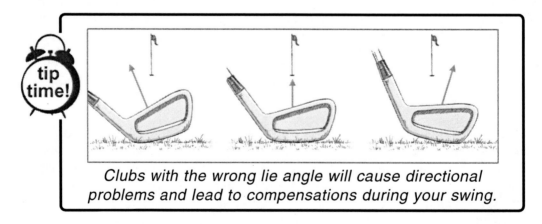

Clubs with the wrong lie angle will cause directional problems and lead to compensations during your swing.

Shafts

You need shafts which are a suitable flex and material for your swing. Flex is the "bendiness" of the shaft. You will want a shaft that bends enough during your normal swing to give your swing some snap, but not so much that it causes inconsistent shots. Typically, shafts which are too stiff feel hard to swing, and cause shots that fly quite low. Shafts that are too flexible, often cause your ball flight to be too high, and can decrease your directional control. Shafts are made out of several substances; the most popular being steel and graphite. The type of shaft that is right for you will be based on your strength. Golfers who need help creating swing speed will benefit from graphite shafts, because they weigh less. Graphite shafts also tends to dampen the vibration caused by impact a little better, so are very good for golfers with joint problems. The potential downsides to graphite are: It is more expensive than steel, and, although the technology of graphite shafts is improving, graphite still performs less consistently than steel. Steel shafts are the choice for golfers strong enough to generate sufficient swing speed, because they perform more predictably.

Grip Size

The thickness of the grips on your clubs needs to be suitable for your hand size and finger length. Grips that are too thick or too thin will cause you to loose control of the club. A properly sized grip will allow the fingers of your top hand to barely reach the fleshy part of your thumb when your grip is completed. Generally speaking, large grips tend to decrease your ability to rotate the clubface through impact while thinner grips promote rotation.

Lofts

The loft of a club is generally only considered when choosing a *driver* or wedges. You need to create certain launch conditions with your tee shots to maximize distance for your swing speed. A driver with too little loft causes too low a launch angle and spin rate, and the ball falls out of the sky prematurely. Too much loft can cause too high a launch, resulting in a waste of energy as the ball climbs too steeply.

Wedges

The choice of which wedges to include in your set is very important. The shots played from within 100 yards of the green will have a large impact on your score. Most sets include a pitching wedge. Another wedge all golfers should have in their bags is a sand wedge, as they are specially designed for use in sand traps.

As with the longer clubs, you should have consistent gaps between each wedge yardage. The gap between the lofts of each iron in a set is 4 degrees. A pitching wedge generally has 48 degrees of loft and the average sand wedge has 56 degrees. This leaves a large gap between the distances you can hit your pitching and sand wedge. Since most golfers aren't comfortable playing partial shots, it is generally a good idea to add a "gap" wedge to your set. Gap wedges have about 52 degrees of loft and will help you avoid the 3/4 pitching wedge shot. Whichever wedges you choose to carry, you should strive to have a 10 - 15 yard difference between the distances each wedge hits the ball.

Putters

As you already know, putting makes up a large percentage of your score. For this reason it is very important for you to have a putter that fits you and that you find comfortable. I am always amazed at how many of my students come to me with putters that are not well suited to them or their putting strokes.

Putters are built differently than other clubs because the putting motion is different. Putters are usually built with between 3 and 7 degrees of loft. This loft helps get the ball on top of the grass but not visibly into the air. The grip is generally flat on top to promote the proper grip with both thumbs on top of the handle. The lie angle is significantly more upright than other clubs, allowing you to

Find a putter that looks and feels good to you and stick with it.

stand more over the ball. This promotes a rocking motion, rather than a turning of the shoulders, and keeps the putter swinging on the target line. Let's look at the customizable characteristics of the putter.

Length

It has been my experience that a large percentage of golfers are using putters that are too long for them. A putter that is too long causes problems at set-up and with the stroke. It forces you to either stand too far from the ball or to create angles at your wrists and elbows. Both situations make it difficult to learn a reliable stroke.

The easiest way to decide on the proper length of putter is to assume your putting stance and find a putter that reaches between your hands. The ideal putting set-up has the arms hanging straight down from the shoulders and the eyes positioned directly over the ball. Picture 1 on the opposite page shows the set-up with a proper length putter. Pictures 2 and 3 show the unwanted effects on the set-up caused by a putter that is too long.

Lie Angle

When a golfer is in an optimal set-up and the handle is between his or her hands, the putter should sit flat on the ground. In this position it will be aiming correctly and will promote solid contact with the ball.

A Putter that Fits You

A putter that fits you will promote a good set-up with your arms hanging straight down and eyes directly over the ball as in picture 1.

Pictures 2 and 3 show when a putter is too long, the ball is played too far from you, or unwanted angles are created at the elbows and wrists.

Head Design

Putters come in many designs with various shapes and with various alignment aids. It is important for you to find a putter style, which you find easy to aim. Some people prefer a rectangular shape, while others like a more rounded head. Some golfers like lines on the putter and others like a clean look. The important thing is to find a putter that you can aim easily and gives you confidence. The ability to properly aim your putter is vital.

Feel

Putters come in different weights. Find one that has the weight and balance you like. It is now very popular for putters to be made with inserts in the face. The inserts allow manufacturers to make similar looking head styles that feel very different when they strike the ball. It is important that you like the balance of your putter and the feel of the ball coming off the face, so you can learn to control the distance of your putts.

Loft

Putters range in loft from 3 to roughly 7 degrees. Putters with less loft are good for very short cut, fast greens, while putters with more loft are better for slower greens and golfers who like to *forward press* a lot when they putt.

Golf Balls

Nowadays, you need a university degree to keep up with golf ball technology. The basic gist is, beginners will benefit from a lower spin ball with a durable cover. Better players will benefit from a ball that spins more and provides softer feel on shorter shots.

Chapter Summary

There are many pieces of your equipment and they all need to be in good working order if you expect to play your best golf.

- ⌐ Your Brain
- ⌐ Your Body
- ⌐ Your Eyes
- ⌐ Your Golf Equipment

Chapter Six
The Full Swing

If you turn on your TV on Sunday afternoon and watch a professional tournament, you will see players of all different sizes, strengths and body types. As a result, you will see a variety of different looking swings. As different as some of the swings may look, all good swings share certain qualities, which allow the golfers to consistently hit good golf shots.

First, and most importantly, all good swings deliver the golf club to the back of the ball along the target line and with a square clubface. If these conditions are met, a straight golf shot is created. As they say, "the ball doesn't know what your name is, it only knows what the club tells it to do". Regardless of how a swing looks, its quality should be judged by its ability to consistently deliver the club to impact correctly. This is great news for golfers all over the world, as it means learning to swing a golf club correctly, is possible for everyone. All you need is the knowledge of how the club must swing through the ball (information provided in this book) and some time to learn how your body needs to move to make it happen. With this in mind, there are a few qualities that most good swings possess which make consistent results possible.

Almost all consistent swings have three positions, which are fundamentally sound, and make learning to deliver the club to the ball easier. Good swings begin from a quality set-up position. There are exceptions, but most good golf swings start with a good hold on the club, an athletic and balanced posture, proper ball position and impeccable aim and alignment.

The top of the backswing position is also very important. Good swingers finish their backswings in good balance with their upper bodies coiled against the resistance of their lower body. Their arms and club are in positions, which allow them to swing the club directly into the back of the ball, towards the target and into balanced finish positions.

Every good swing is in balance with a tempo that fits the golfer's personality. If you are a fast walker and fast talker, your natural tempo is probably fairly quick. Trying to go against this natural sense of time by swinging slowly will cause you problems.

The set-up, backswing and finish form the framework of the swing. The main question is, will your positions allow you to learn the targeting skills needed to play your best golf.

A good golf swing has a solid framework comprised of a good set-up, backswing and finish position. This foundation, combined with an understanding of the key concepts of how the club should be used and plenty of practice will lead to success.

tip time!

One very important point I would like to make off the top is that <u>everyone</u> can set-up to a golf ball effectively, if they choose to spend time learning the fundamentals. <u>Everyone</u> can also learn to make a good backswing based on their body type and physical limitations, if they invest the effort to build the necessary habits. This quality preparation, and a forward swing that ends in a balanced finish will let you apply the swing concepts from Chapter Two and learn the necessary targeting skills that send the ball to the target.

Many golfers fail to ever learn a good swing because they don't initially understand the main concepts that govern how the club must behave through impact. Being clear on the direction you are trying to swing the golf club during the forward swing, will have a big effect on what you try to do during your backswing. If your concept of the forward swing is faulty, your entire swing will be based on these incorrect assumptions, and you are destined to be frustrated for the majority of your golfing life.

If you don't have a firm grasp on the main swing concepts described in Chapter Two, I urge you to re-read that chapter before you move forward.

On the following pages are photos of my golf swing. They will help illustrate some of the points from this chapter. After the swing photos, I will describe the key parts of the swing and the best way to put them together for a repeating motion that you can use to hit consitently good golf shots.

The Set-Up

Take Away

Checkpoint 1

Checkpoint 2

Top of Swing

Transition

Delivery

Impact

Follow Through

Near Finish

The Finish

Before we move forward to learning the swing, I would like to outline my approach to the swing again. The framework of the golf swing is made up of three main positions: the set-up, the top of the backswing and the finish. These are the key points that form the general appearance of the swing. Every swing has these three positions and their quality will help determine a golfer's ability to learn how to hit good golf shots.

I view the set-up and backswing as preparation for hitting a golf shot, while targeting happens in the forward swing. This separation is at the heart of my approach to learning the swing. The fastest and most effective way to learn the golf swing would be to spend sufficient time learning the preparation skills to turn them into habits, before you even looked at a golf ball. The golf ball would be introduced to provide feedback, as you learned what I refer to as the targeting skills: solid contact, clubface control and swing path.

You will struggle if you attempt to learn both parts of the swing at once. When you are working on your preparation, you should not be worried where the golf ball is going. When you are trying to improve your targeting skills, your mind should be free of set-up and backswing thoughts. The consistency of your golf shots will depend on your understanding of the key targeting concepts, the quality of your set-up and backswing, and the amount of time you choose to spend developing your targeting skills.

Preparation – The Set-Up Position

As the title of this section indicates, I view the set-up position as part of the preparation phase of the golf swing. I also view the backswing as part of the preparation phase. In all other sports, the backswing is completed without thought. It is something you do as you get ready to strike a shot or hit a ball. Good preparation makes the actual task easier to execute. In the case of the golf swing, good preparation, with sound pre-shot fundamentals, makes the learning of the targeting skills, required for hitting good golf shots, much easier.

Pre-shot fundamentals are comprised of everything you do before you set the club in motion. A good set-up position gives you an excellent chance to develop a good golf swing. A poor set-up will make it nearly impossible for you to learn an effective and repeating swing motion. Put simply, if you set up to the golf ball poorly, you will need to make compensations during your swing, to hit the ball straight. Compensations are never as reliable as the more natural movements made possible by a good set-up.

The way you place your hands on the club, how you stand, where you place the golf ball in relation to your feet, and how you align your body are all key ingredients for giving yourself the best chance to make a good swing. A technically sound address position also makes the feedback you get from the ball accurate and that feedback plays a big part in the learning process.

The following pages offer general set-up instructions. It is very common for golfers, because of physical situations, such as large chests, big bellies, or injuries, to customize their start positions to accommodate their particular situation. Some general advice for dealing with physical challenges is given later in the chapter.

The Grip

How you place your hands on the club is easily the most important skill you can acquire. A good grip will put your hands on the club with the back of your top hand, the palm of your bottom hand, and the clubface, all facing in the same direction. This symmetry will encourage the clubface to face the target as you learn to return your hands to a position square to the target at impact. You already have the skill needed to face your hands in desired directions, so, creating a relationship between your hands and the clubface will allow you to control the clubface and learn the golf swing more quickly. A good grip will also set the stage for your wrists to work correctly and make a powerful swing possible. This hinging action of the wrists is one of your biggest power sources, so your hands must be oriented correctly so you can access the clubhead speed created by the cocking and uncocking of your wrists during the golf swing.

Most people hold the club too much in the palms of their top hand, resulting in the hands being turned too far to the left for a right-handed golfer (picture 1). This promotes an open clubface and a slice. The correct hold on the club results in the hands facing in the same direction as the clubface, and being turned more to the golfer's right (picture 2).

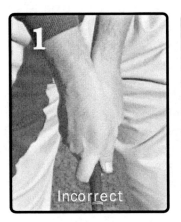

Holding the club in the palm of the top hand causes a "weak" grip, like in picture 1. Holding the club in your fingers will produce a good grip like in picture 2.

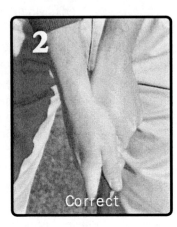

The Top Hand

Most beginner golfers place the golf club too much in the palm of the top hand (picture A below). As a result, the back of the hand isn't in sync with the clubface, and the wrist is out of position. A correct grip will have the handle placed in the fingers of the top hand with the handle running from the base of the index finger under the heel pad (Picture B).

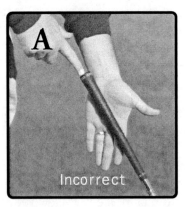

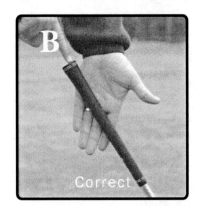

From this position, you can close your fingers and hand around the golf club. This should result in:

- the heel pad being on top of the handle
- the wrist joint located over top of the handle
- the thumb positioned on top of the handle

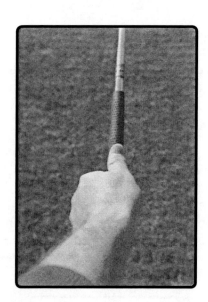

Here is a look at a good top hand grip from the golfer's view. It shows the wrist joint positioned directly over the handle.

The Bottom Hand

The bottom hand needs to mesh with the top hand to create a cohesive unit, and have the palm facing in the same direction as the clubface. You accomplish these two things by placing the thumb pad of your bottom hand over your top thumb, and then wrapping your fingers around the club. Notice, in the completed grip in picture 1, how the thumb of the bottom hand is positioned on the side of the handle and not on top, as many beginners like to do. Also, picture 2 shows a good relatinship between the right hand and clubface. This relationship is key to controlling the clubface. Many people ask me about the pinky finger of the bottom hand. There are three options: putting it on the handle, interlocking it with the forefinger of the top hand, and overlapping it over the forefinger of the top hand. I have no preference, choose the option which is most comfortable to you and stick with it.

One final note about your hands. It is very common to hold the club too tightly. Your hands should be relaxed, so tension will not spread to your arms and into your shoulders. Muscle tension does not allow for fluid motion, so work on keeping your grip pressure at around 3 or 4 on a 10 point scale with 10 being a vice grip!

Posture

Posture is a word that describes body positioning. The golf ball is on the ground, so you must bend over in some way to swing at the proper level. It is important to bend over the correct way, so you can promote proper motion and protect your back from injury. You set your posture by tilting at the hips, maintaining a straight spine and unlocking your knees. This good posture allows your upper and lower body to work together. Picture 1 below shows excellent posture. Pictures 2 and 3 show two common problems I see with posture: too much knee bend, and burying the head in the chest, causing a rounded back.

Picture 1 shows good posture with a straight back and unlocked knees.

Pictures 2 and 3 show the faults of too much knee bend and a rounded back with a buried chin.

Good posture will also put you in good balance. You should feel your weight evenly distributed between the heels and balls of your feet. To check your posture use a mirror to make sure your shoulder joints are over your knees and balls of your feet. If you hang a golf club from your right shoulder joint, the shaft should hang down the back of your arm, and the extension of the vertical line should pass through the tip of your knee cap and into the ground just behind the ball of your foot. This position is like the ready positions you see in other sports like baseball and tennis.

Once you have achieved good posture, it becomes easy to determine your distance from the ball. Golf clubs are built, so that regardless of their length, the end of the grips all end at the same point. This fact allows you to use the same posture for all clubs. If you stand the same distance from every club, the clubs will determine your proper distance from the ball. For most golfers, this distance should be between 1 and 2 hand widths between the butt of the club and your legs (picture below), depending on your body type. Alterations need to be made by golfers with large chests and/or big bellies. If you are the proud owner of a large chest or belly, the key to your posture will be tilting enough at the hips to allow your arms to hang over your physical attribute. Many golfers make the mistake of letting their arms hang beside the body, and it results in the arms having to swing out and around the body during the take away, rather than more straight back.

Distance from the ball and proper ball position between your feet are dictated by the club you are using.

tip time!

Ball Position

Like your distance from the ball, the clubs dictate where the ball should be positioned between your feet. Start with the ball in the middle of your stance for the shorter clubs, like your wedge or 9-iron. As the clubs get longer, move the ball forward until it is positioned opposite the instep of your front foot for your woods.

A longer answer describes why you should change your ball position depending on the club. As I discussed in the section on solid contact, the ability to correctly locate the bottom of your swing is the key to hitting the ball with the centre of the clubface. When using an iron or wood to hit the ball off the ground, the bottom of your swing arc should happen after contact with the ball.

Ideally, if you are a right-handed golfer, the bottom of your swing will happen when your left arm and club shaft form a vertical line. This should happen roughly in front of the left arm pit, where the left arm is in a straight down position. With your feet, shoulder width apart, the left arm pit will be over the inside of your left foot, so you can use your left instep as a good reference point for the bottom of your swing.

Golf clubs are designed to work best at different points in the swing arc. Short irons are built with the shaft leaning substantially towards the target, and should strike the ball well before the bottom of the swing arc. As your clubs get longer, they are built with progressively less shaft lean, and should strike the ball nearer the bottom of the swing (the left instep). By positioning the ball in the middle for the wedges, and moving the ball gradually forward as you use longer and less lofted clubs, you are promoting the proper angle of approach for each club.

tip time! *Position the ball in the middle of your stance for your wedges, and move it progressively foward as the clubs get longer. Finish with the ball even with your front instep when hitting a driver.*

Aim and Alignment

To promote straight golf shots, you need to AIM your clubface and ALIGN your body correctly. A properly aimed clubface has its *leading edge* perpendicular to the target line. To align your body, you need to have your feet, knees, hips, and shoulders positioned parallel to the target line. A great way to remember the alignment concept is to think of railroad tracks. You aim your clubface down one track towards the target, and stand on the other track. This position promotes a square clubface at impact and a proper swing path along the target line. A great way to learn proper aim and alignment is to place golf clubs on the ground as a reminder of good alignment when you practice. This will teach you how proper alignment should look and feel. You should always practice with alignment aids on the ground to build good alignment habits and learn a swing from the same orientation to the target for each shot.

Good alignment means your body lines are parallel to the target line.

Before I go into the second part of your preparation, the backswing, I would like to repeat a major point I made earlier. I do not think the golf swing can be effectively learned by reading about it in a book. I believe you will improve the quality of your swing more quickly by receiving personalized instruction from a qualified PGA Teaching Professional. Having said that, I am going to offer some basic instruction and a couple of checkpoints you can use to build a good backswing.

More Preparation - The Backswing

The backswing is the second part of the preparation phase of the golf swing. Like the set-up position, the quality of your backswing will have a big impact on how consistently you strike the golf ball. The backswing should serve two purposes. First, it should allow you to gather potential energy that can be used in the forward swing for clubhead speed. Secondly, the backswing should end with your golf club in the best possible position to allow for a direct path to the target through the golf ball.

Ideally, your backswing will be a motion you can make without conscious thought. When you are attempting to hit the ball to the target, you will need all of your focus to be on the target, and not on what your body should be doing during your backswing.

The Backswing - The Parts

There are two main movements that make up the backswing: the body turn, and the arm swing. In the golf swing, it is the body's job to create the "AROUND" part of the swing, which takes the club behind the golfer. It is the arms' and wrists' job to swing the golf club UP during the backswing. When the two parts are correctly blended together, the movement of the club will be on a consistent tilt up and around your body on what is called the *swing plane*. Swinging the golf club back "on plane" will make it considerably easier for you to consistently swing the golf club towards the target during the forward swing.

The Body Turn

When isolating the body turn, as in the pictures below, your torso should turn 90 degrees while maintaining your original spine tilt. Your hips and lower body should only turn as much as is necessary to allow the torso to complete its turn.

Completed body turn from two angles.

Notice in the pictures how an effective body turn will satisfy these criteria:

- From an athletic, tilted set-up position, my torso turns 90 degrees while maintaining my original spine tilt.
- The flex in my right knee is maintained.
- The completion of the turn results in my back facing the target.
- My hips do not slide sideways; they turn in place, as my torso turns.
- My head is free to move slightly laterally to accommodate the turning of my body into an athletic position over my right leg.

- At completion of the turn, my sternum is positioned over the inside of my right knee, locating roughly 75 - 80% of my body weight over the inside of the right foot. Note: The shifting of the weight is caused entirely by the turning of the torso and not a conscious shifting of the weight to the right leg by the golfer.
- Depending on the golfer's flexibility, his or her hips will turn between 20 and 60 degrees in response to the turning of the torso.

The Arm Swing

The ideal arm swing will result in the arms and wrists swinging the club up into a position over top of a right-handed golfer's right shoulder joint.

Completed arm swing from two angles.

The picture shows these key elements of the arm swing:

- My wrists create a 90-degree angle between the club shaft and my left arm.
- The shaft of my golf club ends up in position over top of my right shoulder joint.
- My arms have remained extended from the chest with my right arm never bending past a 90-degree angle at the elbow.
- My arms are positioned under the club shaft supporting the weight of the club easily. My elbows are not "flying" away from the body in any way.
- My arms have remained in front of my chest. When the arms get involved in the around part of the swing, the left arm moves across the chest.

The Backswing - Putting it Together

The skills of turning the body and swinging the club up with the arms and wrists are not difficult on their own. It is with the blending together that most golfers struggle. Almost every golfer I see, runs into problems with one of their body parts getting involved with another body part's job. For example, it is very common for golfers to swing the club away from the ball by dragging it too far *inside*. Golfers tend to do this when they are trying to promote an inside-to-out approach to the ball during the forward swing. Unfortunately, the opposite usually happens. When you take the club away from the ball on too far an inside track, you almost always lift the club dramatically during the final part of the backswing. The momentum created by this lifting motion carries the club *"over the top"*, and causes an outside-to-in swing path.

In the case of the club being swung too far to the inside during the take away, you could say the arms are getting involved with the around part of the swing, which is the body's job. When the arms start doing the body's job, the club ends up swinging out of position, and problems arise. Our job as golfers is too blend the two motions together so the club will swing back in the correct amounts of up and around, creating the "on plane" swing, which makes it easier to hit "on target" shots.

To help blend the two motions together, I use a couple of "checkpoints" at key points in the backswing.

A common problem is swinging the club away from the ball too much to the inside. This almost always causes problems later in the swing.

Checkpoint One

At "Checkpoint One", the club has reached
waist height. Your ability to swing the club
back through this position is critical. If the
club is out of position at waist height, you
will really struggle to return the club to
impact successfully. At this point, there are
a few things you can notice about my body
and club positions:

- The club shaft is roughly parallel to the ground.
- The club shaft is parallel to the target line and is positioned over top of my toe line.
- The leading edge of the clubface is parallel to my spine tilt and not straight up and
  down, as a lot of people think it should be. Straight up and down is actually an
  open clubface at this point of the swing.
- The triangle formed by my arms and chest at set-up is still intact. If the arms get too
  involved, the left arm will begin to cross over the chest rather than maintaining its
  original orientation.
- My body weight is beginning to move onto my right leg.

Checkpoint Two

"Checkpoint Two" occurs when the arms reach
parallel to the ground and the golf club is vertical.
Points to notice about this position are:

- My body turn is almost complete.
- My arm swing is almost complete.
- The club shaft and my left arm have
  formed a 90-degree angle.
- My hands are in front the right part of my chest.
- The shaft of the club is pointing towards the target line or ball in this picture.
- Right arm forms at least a 90-degree angle (not collapsing).
- Left arm is extended but not rigid.
- Right elbow is pointing down towards the ground, not flaring out behind me.
  Remember the arms' and wrists' job is swinging the club up, not around.

Checkpoint Three

"Checkpoint Three" is the finished backswing. It happens when the body turn and arm swing are completed. Each golfer's body type will play a large roll in determining the length of his or her backswing. Many golfers try to exceed what their bodies can do, and make too long a backswing by collapsing their arms or loosening their hold on the club at the top of the swing. When your body stops

turning, your arms should stop swinging. The forward swing needs to be a well synchronized motion, so if the arms stop swinging up at the same time the body stops turning, the forward swing will be much easier to blend together.

Body Type Considerations

A quick look around will remind you, we are not all built alike. There are notable differences between the female and male anatomy, and people of the same gender vary drastically in terms of flexibility, strength, and general health. My advice for getting personalized instruction holds even more water if you are a golfer who must deal with a physical situation, such as a large chest, big belly, or limited range of motion. If one of these terms describes your situation, here are a couple of general suggestions, which may help.

Limited Flexibility in Your Back or Neck

To help promote a full body turn, alter your start position by either turning your back foot out slightly or pulling it back a few inches from the target line. These adjustments will free up your right hip to turn a little bit more and help increase your body turn.

Big Chest or Belly

If you have a large chest or belly, ensure your arms are hanging down OVER your chest or belly at set-up. You must tilt more at the hips while maintaining balance and will need to stand further from the golf club. This allows your arms and body to work together as you begin your backswing. The tendency is to let the arms hang to the side of the chest or belly, which forces the arms to swing up and away to avoid the body at the start of the backswing. This almost always results in problems with the blending of arm swing and body turn.

Faults and Fixes

Reverse Weight Shift

The reverse weight shift is a situation where, during the backswing, a golfer's weight shifts onto the front leg instead of the rear leg. This fault is often caused by attempts to keep the head still. Allowing the head to move freely, and learning the proper body turn, will eliminate the reverse weight shift and make a powerful forward swing possible. Often, golfers who find it difficult to transfer their weight in the forward swing, have made a reverse weight shift during the backswing.

Overswing

An overswing is a situation where the golfer swings the golf club back too far. It is often caused by the idea that the farther back he or she swings the club, the farther they will hit the ball. Attempts to make a longer swing, cause the arms to collapse or the hold on the club to loosen, resulting in loss of swing speed and loss of control over contact. A lot of distance is lost by hitting the ball off center, so if you want to hit the ball your farthest, swing within yourself and strive for solid contact. When your body stops turning, your arms should stop swinging the club back. This will make the body and arms easier to synchroinize in the forward swing.

Collapsing Arms

Collapsing arms in the backswing can also be caused by the golfer's inability to properly hinge his or her wrists. A poor hold on the club, with the wrist of the top hand positioned to the side of the club, rather than on top, can make it impossible for the wrists to hinge. This results in the arms hinging to swing the club up instead of the wrists.

Body Sway

The exaggerated hip slide shown in the picture to the right, is usually caused by golfers' attempts to "shift their weight" to the back foot. This causes them to slide their hips laterally and creates real problems by impeding an effective body turn. A good weight shift will happen as a result of a proper body turn when your chest turns over top of the inside of your rear foot.

Targeting - The Forward Swing

The ultimate test of a golf swing's quality is its ability to consistently return the clubface to the back of the ball correctly, and hit golf shots towards the target. I refer to the skills needed to hit a golf ball to your target as, fittingly enough, "Targeting". Learning the targeting skills is dependent on three things:

1. understanding the concepts regarding the correct behavior of the club through impact (Chapter Two)

2. possessing adequate set-up and backswing skills to allow you to develop the targeting skills and reach your desired proficiency level

3. spending enough practice time to learn the targeting skills

Notice I didn't mention needing to understand when to turn your hips, or when to uncock your wrists, or anything like that. Many golfers attempt to understand all the parts of the forward swing and struggle to perform. In special cases, I will work with a student on specific parts of their forward swing, but in general, I avoid breaking the forward swing into parts. The elapsed time between the end of the backswing and impact is between .20 and .25 of a second, depending on the golfer. An awful lot of movements have to happen in that short period of time to hit a good golf shot!

Rather than focussing on all the little things that need to happen to successfully deliver the club to the back of the ball, I rely on the brain's ability to control the hands. A large portion of your brain is dedicated to fine motor skills, namely your hands. I believe your brain will make the necessary calculations regarding body movement if it understands how the club relates to your hands (discussed in Chapter Two), and where you are trying to swing the golf club. All of the motions like weight shift, hip rotation, right elbow movement, etc., will be learned automatically, and will be based on what your body is capable of doing, not what some tour pro does.

The reason professional golfers of different body types and with different looking swings can all hit long and straight golf shots, is they have learned world class targeting skills. In short, they have learned how they each need to swing the club so it performs correctly as it swings through the golf ball. They fully understand the necessary concepts and they have learned how their particular bodies must move to make the club behave correctly. In many cases, the best golfers aren't the ones who understand how the golf swing works, they are the ones who understand how their body works best to hit good golf shots. What Tiger, Ernie or Phil do should be irrelevant to you, as you learn your best swing.

It is my hope, after having read Chapter Two, that you now understand the important targeting concepts. With this knowledge in place, you can put your swing to the test. If you know what the club should be doing to cause straight golf shots, can you make it happen? In other words, will the quality of your preparation (set-up position and backswing), allow you to deliver the club to the ball correctly? If the answer is yes, terrific. If the answer is no, you may need to improve the quality of your preparation so you can learn targeting skills that you will deem satisfactory.

Targeting skills need to be learned, so it may take a few practice sessions to see improvement in the quality of your shots even if your preparation is satisfactory. I recommend you get professional instruction on what parts of you swing need improving. Your teacher can give you important feedback on whether you need to improve your preparation, or continue practicing your targeting skills. It is a Teaching Professional's job to diagnose your swing problems so you can focus your practice effectively. Trying to fix swing problems on your own may result in many hours of wasted efforts working on the wrong things. I have included an entire chapter on how to practice, starting on page 151, but here are some thoughts on practicng your swing.

Learning the Swing

In a perfect world, golfers would learn their swings in a room with mirrors and no golf balls. Once they had the basic swing practiced, and to the point of being an automatic habit, they would use golf balls to learn the targeting skills. Many golfers struggle because they try to learn the preparation skills while focussing on the targeting outcomes of each shot. This is the ultimate reason golfers struggle to learn a swing or make improvements to their existing swings.

The set-up and backswing are best learned through large numbers of repetition until you can perform them without the need for thought. Once you have an understanding of the correct positions or movements required, it is your goal to make the preparation phase of your swing an automatic response. The best way to begin learning the preparation part of the swing is to work in front of a mirror where you can see if you are completing the motions correctly.

Practicing in front of a mirror is a great way to learn set-up and backswing habits.

When you have successfully executed enough rehersals in the mirror to accurately feel what you are doing during the backswing, you can then introduce the ball. At this point, as you continue to work on your backswing, you need to remain focussed on the quality of your swing motion and not be distracted by your ball flight. Remember, you are building habits so you can move on to playing golf without having to think about your swing at all. To do this, you will need sufficient repetitions to make your backswing automatic.

The targeting skills of solid contact, squaring the clubface, and the proper swing path will be learned most efficiently after understanding the important concepts outlined in Chapter Two. Study these concepts, and then, start with small swings with a wedge to learn the desired motions through the ball to develop the targeting skills most quickly.

Depending on your present skill level, you may need to isolate each of the three skills to learn them, initially. If this is the case, work on controlling the clubface first, by applying the concept of closing the clubface through impact with the rotation of your forearms. As I described in detail in Chapter Two, you must learn how to control the clubface, by first understanding how the clubface relates to your hands, and then learning to time the closing of the clubface to create a square impact position. This should be your first step, so you can eliminate any scooping action with your hands that would also sabotage your efforts to make solid contact, and swing the club on the proper path.

After you have learned how to control the clubface, you can quickly learn solid contact and the correct swing path. To work on solid contact, the correct location for the bottom of your swing, you will need to focus on where your club is striking the ground. Practicing on a grass driving range is the best way to get accurate feedback about the point where your club stikes the turf. First, put a tee in the ground, barely sticking out above the grass. With a short iron and the tee in the middle of your stance, work on taking a divot just after the tee. When you can do this most of the time, put a ball on the low tee and continue taking shallow divots just after the tee, allowing the ball to get in the way. You will see how the loft of the club propels the ball up into the air when you make a small divot just after impact. After a while, you can eliminate the tee all together and hit balls right off the grass.

I think every golfer can learn to swing the club down the target line and start the ball towards his or her target consistently. To learn this, you must first be able to control the clubface, because without control of the curvature on your golf shots, you will need to use the path of your swing to compensate for your slice or hook.

I have a great drill I use with my students to tie the three targeting skills together. It involves putting a club down behind and out in front of the ball, on the target line. Your job in this drill is to swing the club through the impact zone so the clubhead is travelling down the target line, and squaring-up through impact. To have the club on the proper path, the shaft of the club you are swinging must point out towards the shafts on the ground (the target line) at all times, as the club swings below waist level. It may feel to you like the club is swinging out to the right, but this is how the club needs to swing to be traveling in the correct direction at impact. Most right-handed golfers learn to swing left of the target to counteract a slice, so they have a false perception of the correct path. To monitor your clubface in this drill, the *scoring lines* of the club should always point between your feet.

This drill, pictured below, is great for learning how to control the club in every respect from waist high to waist high during the forward swing.

When the club is below waist level, the shaft should always be pointing out towards the target line.

Begin this drill using a wedge and only a half swing. I am a firm believer that if you can't hit a wedge solidly and straight with a half swing, you shouldn't expect to hit the ball straight with a longer swing. When you can perform the targeting skills with total mastery on shorter swings, you can progress into longer swings with your wedge. When the longer swings with the wedge are working well, you can move into hitting shots with your longer clubs. I recommend you only continue hitting shots with the longer clubs if you are having success. When your shots begin to deteriorate, return to a shorter club or shorter swing until your results improve again. It is very important as you build the foundation of your golf swing, that you make the correct motions and gain confidence in your abilities. Shorter swings will give you both.

Check your pre-shot fundamentals at the beginning of every practice session. It is vital that your grip, posture, ball position, and alignment remain constant. Use a practice station with clubs on the ground, at all times, to maintain the integrity of your set-up position. After a swing has been built, the main reason golfers run into problems is carelessness with their pre-shots fundamentals, which leads to swing changes. If you begin hitting poor shots, always check your set-up position first. A long and frustrating search for a swing flaw that isn't there can be avoided with a correction to one of your pre-shot fundamentals.

tip time!

When practicing your targeting skills, always use alignment aids on the ground to ensure your aim and alignment are correct.

It is my belief the targeting skills are in a constant state of fine-tuning depending on how you are feeling on any given day, or how much you are getting a chance to play.

Faults and Fixes

Over the Top

Over the top is a term used to describe a swing flaw, which sends the club outside and over top of the ideal plane at the start of the forward swing. This swing fault causes the club to swing from outside-to-in at the bottom of the swing, and results in a shot that starts left of the intended target for right-handed golfers.

Much is written about how to fix this very common problem, but I feel you need to understand why you do it before you can actually fix it. I believe all golfers have the ability to swing the golf club towards the target. There are two main reasons golfers don't do it:

1. The tendency for golfers to try to create power with their upper bodies, resulting in the torso being far too active at the beginning of the forward swing.

2. The second, and most common, is they have learned to swing the club from outside-to-in because their club is usually open at impact.

Let me explain. The majority of golfers take to the game with at least a couple of misconceptions that promote a slice. They generally have a poor grip that promotes an open clubface at impact, and they typically misunderstand the concept of how to square the clubface during the swing. The result is a steady diet of golf shots that slice. After watching ball after ball slice to the right, they begin to do the inevitable, swing the club over the top so it will swing to the left through impact. This is a completely logical reaction to shots that are curving to the right of the target.

This desire to swing the club to the left causes the golfer to come over the top. What makes it worse is, when the golfer does this, his or her ball generally finishes closer to the hole, so they think they are improving. What they have actually done is learned a new swing fault to compensate for their original swing fault. Two wrongs can make a right but in this case, it will take significantly more practice to perfect the compensations than it will to learn how to swing the club towards the target.

To fix the over the top move, you must eliminate the initial reason for it by learning to control the upper body at the start of the forward swing and/or developing the ability to control the clubface so it returns to a square position at impact. Only after you can hit the golf ball fairly straight, without a lot of curvature, can you learn to correct your swing path by eliminating the over the top move. When the ball flies fairly straight, the game becomes easy, because all you have to worry about is swinging the stick towards the target and you already know how to do that.

You would have to be crazy to swing the club towards the target if you thought the ball was going to curve to the right! In fact, the only way you can completely eliminate the over the top move is to develop confidence in your ability to square the clubface. If you have doubts about whether the ball will fly straight, you will always tend to swing to the left.

Take it from a reformed slicer; you need to fix the curve on your ball before you can make corrections to the swing path. Attempting to fix your outside-to-in swing path, before you have control over the clubface, will result in a long and frustrating process and you will never completely eliminate the over the top swing from your game.

" *You Lifted Your Head* "

Many people think topped shots happen because they lift their heads. While a golfer's head may lift, the actual cause of topped shots is usually his or her attempts to help lift the ball into the air with the swing. This leads to the destructive tendency of locating the bottom of the swing behind the ball and causes topped and fat shots. Spend some time learning to swing the club down through the ball, locating the bottom of your swing just after impact and those topped shots will be gone forever. Coincidentally enough, your head will stop popping up during your swing!!

Topped or Fat Shots

Topped or thin shots happen when the bottom of your swing is in the wrong place relative to the ball. If you are having problems with making solid contact, ensure the ball is positioned properly in your stance and then practice until you can consistently make your swing bottom out correctly. For all shots played off the ground, your swing needs to contact the ground just after the ball. For balls played off tees, your club should strike the ball while traveling level to the ground or slightly up into the ball. To accomplish this, your swing needs to bottom out right at or slightly before the ball. This is a skill that needs to be learned through practice. Many golfers incorrectly blame the lifting of their head for topped shots and the dropping of the rear shoulder for fat shots. These problems during the forward swing are only symptoms of the real problem, trying to help the ball into the air.

The Slice

The slice is caused by an open clubface. To eliminate the slice from your game you will need to learn how to square the clubface at impact. If you hold the club correctly, understand the concepts discussed in Chapter Two, and spend time practicing, you can learn to hit the ball straight. Remember to start with smaller swings until you can hit the shorter shots straight, and then make progressively longer swings.

Chapter Summary

- The set-up, backswing and finish positions make up the framework of the swing.

- The set-up and backswing are the preparation phase of the swing.

- The forward swing is the targeting phase.

- The targeting skills of solid contact, clubface control and proper swing path can be learned when the concepts are understood and the framework of the swing is fundamentally sound.

- Ideally, you will learn the framework of the swing without golf balls and introduce the ball to practice your targeting skills.

Putting accounts for nearly 40% of your strokes but it is far more important than that. If you are putting well, it takes the pressure off the rest of your game and lets you make good decisions.

Chapter Seven
Putting

Putts account for close to a third of your score. The ability to consitently putt well is critical to your development as a golfer. The most important skills in putting are:

- making almost all of your putts from within four feet of the cup
- making your share of putts from ten feet and closer to the hole
- rarely needing three or more putts to get the ball in the hole from longer range

As you will see in Chapter Twelve on what to practice, I give putting credit for about one third of your final score. In reality, putting is much more important than that, because it is your last shot on each hole and has the ability to either save your bacon when you make a good putt, or demoralize you when you miss a short one.

Putting affects your entire game. When you are putting well, your shots around the green are made easier, because you don't feel you need to get the ball really close to the hole to make a saving putt. You don't feel pressure on your iron shots, because you know you can recover from a poor shot. The ability to make putts even makes your tee shots easier because you know you can sink a long putt to make up for a stray tee shot.

Conversely, there is nothing worse than hitting a great shot, right up close to the hole and failing to take advantage of it by missing a short putt. If this happens a few times, you may start to put pressure on yourself to get your shots closer to the hole. This added pressure often results in an increased number of poor shots.

I think you get my point. If you want to become a better golfer and get the most out of your game, you need to become a better than average putter.

Like the full swing; the quality of a putting stroke is judged by its ability to roll the ball in the intended direction. There are many different kinds of putters, and almost as many ways to hold them. If you are getting good results with your current putting style, I would not recommend making any changes to your approach. My recommendations are based on the fundamentals most good putters use, and are by no means the only effective way to putt. Good putters have generally experimented a lot with their technique over time before settling on the way that gives them the best results.

The putting stroke is different than any other motion in the game. The ideal stroke will swing the putter back and through along the target line with the putterface remaining relatively square to the target line throughout the motion. A technically sound stroke will allow you to make consistently solid contact and control the direction of your putts. It will also make it possible for you to learn how to govern the speed of your putts, which is one of the most critical skills needed to become a proficient putter.

The Set-Up

The set-up position for putting will be similar to your full swing set-up with a couple of exceptions. Your hold on the putter is typically different and you you will stand more over top of the ball. As with the full swing, you need to establish good posture, aim, and alignment. Your ability to properly aim the putterface is especially critical to your putting success.

The conventional putting grip will position the handle in the palms of the hands with the thumbs of both hands placed on top of the handle. This grip creates a good relationship between the hands and the putterface, and discourages unwanted wrist action during the stroke.

Your posture should be very similar to the full swing with a nice tilt at the hips and a straight spine providing clearance for your arms so they can hang down from your chest. This tilted position, combined with the putter's very upright lie angle, makes it possible for you to stand much closer to the ball. Your set-up should locate your eyes directly over or just inside the target line. This will let you look down your intended line, helping you align more easily.

The most important part of your putting set-up is the aiming of your putterface. A square putterface at set-up will make it more likely for you to return it to square at impact, and the orientation of the putterface at impact has the biggest effect on a putt's initial direction.

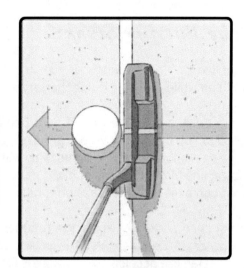

The most important factor in putting is the direction the putter is facing at impact.

Notice in the pictures these important points of a good putting set-up:

- good posture with my spine straight and arms hanging clear from my body
- my arms hanging straight down with no angles created at my elbows or wrists
- my palms facing with my right hand facing in same direction as the putterface
- my eyes over or just inside the target line and behind the ball
- my toes, knees, hips, shoulders, forearms, and eyes all parallel to the intended start line of the putt
- the ball is positioned just inside my left foot to promote a level angle of approach of the putter to the ball

The Putting Stroke

Just like for the full swing, our goal in putting is to have the putter make solid contact with the ball while swinging along the target line and facing the target at impact.

The stroke is often described as a pendulum-like motion of the arms and shoulders. A good set-up position with your arms hanging straight down from your chest, will promote a rocking motion of the shoulders. This will swing the arms and keep the putter head on the target line throughout the stroke. The stroke should be free of any appreciable wrist action that can alter the putterface orientation, and make distance control harder to learn.

Most good putters have strokes that have backswings and forward swings of roughly the same length. Common mistakes include backswings that are too short, resulting in a hurried, almost jab-like acceleration during the forward swing, or an overly long backswing, resulting in the need to decelerate through impact. Both of these situations generally result in considerable loss of directional and distance control.

Direction Control

There are a few factors, which will dictate your ability to roll putts in the direction you have picked. If a putter is miss-aimed at impact, almost all of the deviation is transferred to the putt while less than ¼ of any path deviation is imparted on the ball. The final piece of the puzzle might surprise you. If the path and putter aim are both perfect at impact, but the putt is struck more than a ¼ inch off the sweet spot of the putter, you will miss almost every single time from ten feet or further.

Putter Aim

Properly aiming the putterface is vital to good putting, so you must learn to position the putterface at 90-degrees to your intended line, EVERY time. The use of a spot, a short distance in front of your ball on your intended line, or lining up the printing on the ball in the direction you would iike the putt to start, are two popular ways of ensuring your putter is correctly aimed. You can also have a friend or a teaching professional check your aim and help you learn what correct aim looks like when you are in your set-up position.

Your stroke must return the putterface to a square position at impact. A putting motion, which is free from hand, arm, or shoulder rotation will result in the putterface remaining square to the target line throughout the stroke, and most importantly, facing the target at impact. Any movements which cause the putterface to open or close during the backswing will make it much more difficult for the golfer to consistently return the putterface to square at impact.

The Putting Stroke

- ♚ The putting motion is controlled by the arms and shoulders and features no wrist motion.
- ♚ The shoulders rock and create a swinging motion, which keeps the putter swinging back and through on the target line.
- ♚ The putterface is square to the target during most of the stroke.
- ♚ The head and lower body remain very still to ensure solid contact and maintenance of proper swing path.
- ♚ The stroke is virtually the same length back and through.

Path

Even though the path of your putting stroke is not as important as the other two factors, a poor path is enough to cause you to miss putts. Ideally, the putter will be swinging directly down the intended line of the putt as it swings through the ball. The easiest way to promote this motion is to learn how to rock your shoulders, rather than turning them like in the full swing.

Solid Contact

Making solid contact is an often-overlooked skill. Hopefully not anymore, after reading how important it is! The main factors that will dictate your ability to make solid contact have already been covered. A good set-up position combined with a pendulum stroke, void of head and excess body motion, will make it quite easy to learn solid contact.

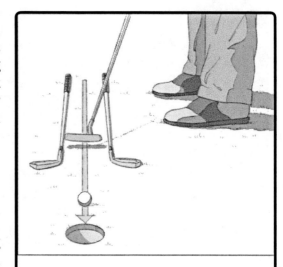

The proper path will result in the putter swinging along the target line.

You will find a few really helpful drills for working on all three of the skills that affect the direction of your putts starting on Page 80.

Many golfers allow their wrists to collapse at impact as in the picture. This causes problems with direction and distance control. Strive to keep your arms and hands swinging to the target as you make your forward stroke. Your left wrist should remain flat, long past impact.

Distance Control

Distance control is an entirely learned skill made easier by a sound and rhythmical putting stroke. There are no words to describe how you can throw a ball the correct distance to a target - you just know. Someone can't tell you how hard to hit a putt, you need to develop feel for distance with your putting so you can judge for yourself how hard to hit each putt.

A stroke that features smooth acceleration and a consistent tempo will make distance control much easier to learn. Ideally your putting stroke will take the same time, regardless of the length of the putt. This is why many golfers find it helpful to practice their putting with a metronome. The steady timing of the metronome helps you learn to use the same rhythm on all putts. Next time you are on the putting green, hit a few putts of different lengths and say "one" as you are making your backswing, and "two" when you are making your forward swing. You may be surprised to discover the closeness of the tempos of each stroke. If they aren't, some practice with a metronome will help.

Using a putter that you like the balance, weight and feel of will really help you develop control over your speed. Being consistent with the kinds of balls you play will also help. By "kinds" I am referring to the construction. Fluctuations in firmness of cover and/or core will leave you guessing how the ball will react off your putter and make it harder for you to have consistency in your feel for distance.

Distance control must be learned through practice. It is made easier with a smooth, accelerating stroke.

A point of interest, the ideal speed for a putt to be traveling, to give it the best chance of going in, would send the ball eighteen inches past the hole if it misses. This speed will keep the ball tracking on line as it slows down, but doesn't shrink the hole by requiring the ball to hit right in the center to go in.

Now that you know a little bit about the putting stroke, let's take a look at some other skills needed to make putts.

Green Reading

Green reading is learned over time with experience and practice. It is a skill that will become increasingly important as your direction and distance control improves.

When trying to determine how much a slope will affect your putt, you must first decide how fast your ball will be rolling on its way to the hole. The slower your ball is rolling, the more slopes will affect its path. This is why you need to consider the speed factors first, and then add in the break factors after you have determined how fast your ball will be rolling.

Speed Factors

The ball will always be rolling at its slowest as it nears the hole, so the slopes nearer the hole will affect the ball more than the ones near the ball. Pay special attention to the final ten feet of the putt when making your decision on line. Other factors, which affect how fast the ball will roll are green speed (length of grass), putting uphill or downhill, putting into the grain or with the grain, moisture level of the greens, and sometimes even wind. Once you have factored all of these variables together, you should have a good idea how hard you will need to hit the putt, and how fast the ball will be rolling as it travels to the hole. It is now time to assess the break factors.

Break Factors

The most obvious break factor is the amount of side slope between the ball and the hole. You may also have to consider the direction of the grain and wind depending on where you are playing. Judging the amount a putt will break is not an exact science, but you will become better at judging slopes as you play more.

General Tips on Reading the Greens

🏴 <u>Start reading the green as you approach from the fairway</u>. You can gain valuable information about a green from further out. Looking at a green from back in the fairway will help you see the big picture of how the green fits into the surrounding terrain. Most golf courses have a consistent slope to the entire property, often running away from a mountain or towards a body of water.

⌨ <u>Pay attention to geographical situations</u>. Many golf courses have a general slope towards or away from an over-riding geographical force. It may be a river or lake alongside the course, or it could be a mountain. If you are playing somewhere new, ask the locals if there are any tricks to the greens

⌨ <u>Watch other players' putts</u>. This only works if you are playing with golfers who have good putting strokes. A bad putter's ball may confuse you, but you can learn a lot by watching other balls rolling on the greens, especially as they slow down.

⌨ <u>Gather information with your feet</u>. You'd be amazed how much your feet can tell you if you listen to them. They can tell you about slopes and also about distance. You don't need to pace off the exact distance, simply walking to the hole and back, will give you a better feel for the distance and slopes.

⌨ <u>Look at the Cup</u>. Quite often you can see a slope by looking at the two edges of the cup. You can generally see if one lip is higher than the other.

⌨ When trying to read big breaking putts, do two things. <u>Figure out where the ball will need to enter the hole based on the slope.</u> View this as the middle of the hole for that putt, and figure out where your ball will have to travel to enter the hole through the revised centre of the cup. This will help you "see" the line.

Secondly, when you are standing behind your ball, try to look down your intended line and not in a straight line between your ball and the hole. <u>Move from side to side until you feel like you are facing in the direction your ball would have to start</u> for the slope to take it to the hole. This will also help you "see" the proper line.

Look down your line rather than towards the hole.

⌨ <u>Watch your ball if it misses the hole.</u> An easy way to read your second putt is to watch how your first putt rolls as it passes the hole.

⌨ Imagine how water would flow if you dumped a big bucket on the green. This will help you find the lowest point of the green and the direction most putts will break.

A Positive Attitude

Not many of us can be positive all the time. A good attitude and confidence are learned. We learn to be positive by anchoring good results and being dispassionate about poor ones. Chapter Nine, on the mental game, offers more on developing a positive attitude.

Success in putting will be made possible by practicing good fundamentals and using practice drills that teach you to expect the ball to go in the hole. The use of a putting routine every time you putt will put your mind at ease when it really matters.

To be a confident putter, you need to make putts. How do you make putts if you're not a confident putter? The answer is you start at a length where you will have success and gradually move out. It is important for you to anchor the good putts and view the missed putts only as data, which will help you learn. This method helps control the images your brain associates with putting and will help you develop a confident attitude.

Oh yeah, one last point on your attitude. It has been my experience that almost all golfers have unrealistic expectations for their putting. It may surprise you to know the average PGA Tour Pro only makes a little over half of his 6-footers. His success rate goes to roughly 20% from ten feet, then drops off the charts from longer range. These are tour professionals who are putting on perfect greens every week. Your expectations can be thrown out of whack because when you watch golf tournaments on TV you see the ten best golfers in the world that week. They are near the lead because they are making all of their six-footers. Try to remember this the next time you get all flustered about missing a six-footer. You need to expect to make every putt yet not get upset when you miss.

Making Putts

Every good putter I have ever met follows the same steps every time he or she attempts a putt. This final piece of the putting puzzle is called a putting routine. It will relax your mind, making it possible for you to make more putts, especially when it matters most.

The best putting routines gather information in an organized way, deciding on the ball's route to the hole, creating a consistent and accurate set-up position, and then freeing the golfer to make his or her best stroke.

If you don't already use a consitent routine when you putt, I advise you to use my suggestions on the next page, to build one. Once your routine is built, use it on every putt on the course and a large percentage of your putts during practice.

I like my students to build a putting routine that includes the following steps:

1. Consider the speed factors and establish a feel for the ideal speed for the putt at hand. (pictures 1 and 2)
2. Use this speed to predict the necessary line to the hole.
3. Become devoted to the selected line. Once it has been selected you must have unwavering commitment to the selected line for the remainder of the routine. Any uncertainty must be dealt with by returning to step one and beginning the routine again.
4. Stand behind the ball and visualize the ball rolling with the correct speed, down the desired line, and dropping into the hole.
5. Go through the physical steps of rehearsing the stroke required for the putt and then move into your set-up position. Your set-up position must position the putter face and your body correctly for the intended line of the putt. (pictures 2 and 3)
6. Once you are in position to make a stroke, focus your mind on the desired speed of the putt. A good set-up and a repeating stroke built with practice will take care of direction, leaving you to focus exclusively on speed during the stroke. (picture 3)
7. Make your stroke with only speed in mind. (picture 4)

A good putting routine should be learned and then used on every putt, even during practice sessions.

I have found that most people become anxious and make poor strokes when they are trying to control both the direction and speed of a putt during the stroke. You need to control the direction by building a repeating stroke that rolls the ball along your intended line and having a sound routine that allows you to consistently set up correctly to that intended line. With the direction control out of the way, you will be free to focus all your attention on the job of rolling the ball at the correct speed.

In short, the routine is SPEED - LINE – SPEED. If you will spend the time to build a good putting routine and commit to using it during practice and play, your putting will improve dramatically, especially on those important putts on the last green.

Practicing Your Putting

Before you begin working on your putting, I suggest you go to Appendix B on page 179 and have a look at the putting evaluation. This will give you an excellent tool for assessing your current skills, and make it fun for you to keep track of your improvement.

Putting practice should take the same form as for the full swing. First, spend time on building a repeating stroke. When you have a repeating stroke, you can begin learning to control direction and distance, and then move on to developing the other putting skills needed for making putts on the course.

Building Your Stroke at Home

Using a mirror will help you check your posture, eye position, and the rest of your set-up position. Use the points from earlier in the chapter to ensure your set-up is sound.

When it's time to build your putting stroke, an excellent way to practice is by making your stroke with your forehead resting gently against a wall. Place a ball a couple of inches from the wall so when you can barely feel the wall against your head, the ball will be directly beneath your eyes. You can then hit some putts. This drill will help you in a number of ways: it makes it easy to learn a square set-up position with a square putter face, it helps you learn to swing the putter straight back and straight through, and it helps eliminate head movement which causes problems with contact and direction. It's a great drill as long as you don't mind being seen by your family with your head against a wall! It's a small price to pay for making more putts.

Practicing your putting indoors, especially in the colder months, is a great way to build or maintain a good putting stroke.

Stroke Drills for the Practice Green

The Putting Track

Practice your putting with clubs on the ground forming a track towards the hole. This will help you aim your putter correctly and is a great way to build a stroke that swings the putter back and through on the target line. Start with the clubs quite far apart and as you get better, move the clubs closer together to provide a challenge. This drill is similar to the wall drill you can use at home.

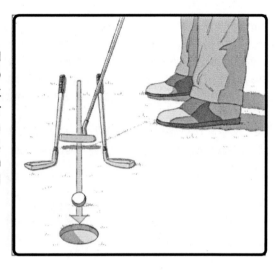

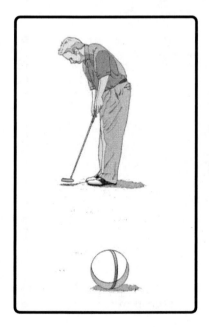

Get the Ball Rolling

The best way to get your ball to stay on line is to get it rolling "end over end" as soon as possible after impact. A great drill to practice this, is to use a range ball with the line positioned on the top of the ball. Your job is to roll the ball so the line stays on top as it travels along. If you can, it means your putterface is square to the target and your path is towards the target at impact. If the line wobbles, you need to spend some time working on your stroke mechanics.

Band-aid Drill

A great drill for working on the quality of your contact, is to place two band-aids on your putter with one on each side of the sweet spot. You can then hit some putts and you will get very clear feedback about what part of the putterface is striking the ball. Learning to hit your putts solidly will help with both direction and distance control.

Learning to Control Distance

Learning to control the distance on your putts is crucial to both making putts and eliminating three-putts. The good news is distance control is a learned skill so everyone can become very skilled in this regard. I have two drills I like my students to work on for developing feel. One is to drop a few balls at one spot and practice by rolling balls to several different holes on the practice green from that one position.

The second is what I call the "Ladder Drill". In the ladder drill you will roll your first putt out about ten feet and then roll every subsequent putt three feet further.

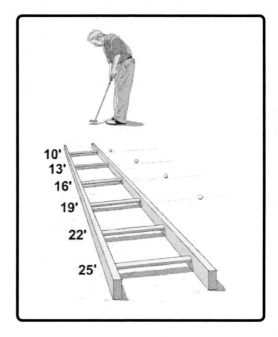

> *The ladder drill is excellent for developing the ability to control distance with your putting stroke.*

Getting Ready for the Course

To get ready for the course you need to make your practice as much like the real thing as possible. The following drills are great because they add a little bit of pressure to your practice and make it more like on the course.

Make 100 in a Row

Just as it sounds, pick a length of putt you feel you can make 100 times in a row. If you are short on time, make it 10 or 20 in a row. The important part is you can't leave the putting green until you accomplish your goal. The last couple of putts will get your attention, just like on the 18th green!

The Line Drill

This great drill, shown in the picture to the right, calls for you to position your balls in a line stretching back from the hole in two or three foot increments. To finish the drill you need to make all of the putts in a row. When you are standing over the last putt, you may feel a little nervous or excited. Sound familiar?

One Ball For Nine Holes

Putt a nine-hole circuit around the practice green. On each putt, go through your routine as you would on the course. Set a goal for your total score. Over time, try to lower your 9-hole scores.

The Compass Drill

This is another one of my favourites. Position your balls at north, south, east and west about two feet from the hole. Your task is to make all four in a row. When you do, move out to three feet and so on. If you make it to ten feet, call me, you're ready for the tour!

Lay Backs

Putt nine holes on the practice green, and each time you miss, pull your ball back from the hole, the length of your putter. This game gives you a steady diet of three and four-footers, the putts you need to make if you want to shoot good scores.

Putt for "Nickels"

Nothing gets your attention like putting for money with friends. Don't make the stakes high enough to hurt anyone, but a little wager will prepare you for the pressure putts you will face on the course.

Have Fun

If you're having fun, you will be improving. Make up your own game or alter these drills to add spice to your practice. Whatever you do, practice your putting a lot!

Chapter Summary

- Like all shots in golf, a good set-up position will make a good putting stroke possible.

- Learn how to aim your putterface correctly every time.

- The stroke should be a rocking motion of the shoulders and not a turning of the torso.

- Your head and lower body should remain still during the stroke.

- A good stroke will let you learn distance control.

- Green reading is a skill that takes time and experience to learn.

- Practice to learn a repeating stoke and then strive to make your practice as much like the course as possible.

- Build and use a putting routine on every putt on the course and most putts during practice.

Chapter Eight
The Scoring Game

I use the term scoring game to describe all shots played to the green from within 75 yards. The scoring game accounts for nearly 20% of your score, so it needs to be practiced on a regular basis. The biggest difference between professional golfers and the average player is efficiency on shots played from close to the green. Professionals regularly take two or fewer shots, while high handicappers often take four or more to get the ball in the hole from relatively short range. I think, if every golfer on the planet took three short game lessons from a teaching professional, golf scores the world over would drop by 5 to 10 shots, almost overnight.

If you are a beginner golfer, your ability to get your ball on the green in one shot from short range, will have positive effects on your scoring. Most beginner golfers struggle with these shots and miss the green a lot of the time, adding several strokes to their scores. To keep improving and become an intermediate player, hitting the green will not be good enough. You will want to get the ball close enough to the hole to one-putt every so often and completely eliminate three-putts by always getting your ball within easy two-putt range.

To become an advanced player, you will need to develop the ability to get your ball within ten feet of the cup, regularly. Ten feet is important because most golfers don't make a high percentage of putts from outside ten feet. To really improve your scoring, you must consistently get the ball within ten feet of the hole or closer to make one-putting realistic.

To become an elite player, you will need to get the ball progressively closer or actually in the hole to increase the number of times you need one or fewer putts. Getting the ball close enough to one-putt is the easiest way to lower your scores.

Your putting skills will play a tremendous role in your scoring. To play your best golf you must eliminate three-putts from long range, and increase your conversion rate from inside ten feet. Even with exceptional putting skills, you will need to get the ball close to the hole with your scoring shots to make one-putting a regular occurence.

Improving your scoring game will go in steps.

Step 1 – Take 4 or less shots to get the ball in the hole from 75 yards and closer.

Step 2 – Take 3 or less shots to get the ball in the hole from 75 yards and closer.

Step 3 – Steadily increase the percentage of times you get the ball in the hole in two shots from within 75 yards until you can do it at a professional level.

Learning the Scoring Game

I break the scoring game down into three levels that need to be learned in order.

⌘ Level One is making consistent contact with the ball, and is dependent on your technique.

⌘ Level Two is controlling how far your ball travels through the air. Feel and control over clubhead speed will dictate how far the ball flies.

⌘ Level Three is controlling how far the ball rolls after it lands. This is accomplished with shot trajectory, the characteristics of your landing zone and backspin.

This chapter focuses on the techniques for the four main shots that make up the scoring game. Chip shots, pitch shots, partial wedge shots, and sand play are the shots you need to learn to be really efficient from within 75 yards of the green.

Every shot in golf has a flight component and a roll component. On the full shots, you control the flight component by selecting the appropriate club for the distance to the target. The roll is predictable by the normal height of your shots and the firmness of the ground where your ball will be landing. The difference in the scoring game is you will need to control the flight component by changing the length and speed of your swing. If you are thinking correctly, you will calculate roll into every shot you play so you can effectively pick the spot where you would like your ball to land.

Level One – Consistent Contact

The biggest problems I see with golfers' scoring games are a poor set-up position and an incorrect swing concept. These lead to inconsistent contact and make the short game impossible to learn. The concepts governing solid contact discussed earlier are especially important in the scoring game. When you can make consistent contact, the short game is fun and easy to learn. Good technique makes solid contact possible when hitting the four main types of scoring game shots: chipping, pitching, partial wedge shots, and sand play.

tip time!

Better Chipping and Pitching

Contact problems in the scoring game often arise from a poor set-up position with the ball too far forward in the stance and a lot of weight on the back foot (picture 1). Fat and thin shots are also caused by trying to scoop the ball into the air with the wrists through impact (picture 2). A proper set-up position and technique that creates solid contact, letting the loft of the club get the ball in the air will make your short game more reliable and lower your scores.

Chipping

The chip is a shot played within close range of the green. The ball spends very little time in the air and most of its time rolling along the ground. The most common causes of poor chipping, pictured on the previous page, are a faulty set-up and a scooping action with the wrists through impact in an attempt to lift the ball into the air.

The Set-Up

The set-up for this shot is designed to promote a descending blow to the ball, making clean and solid contact more likely. The key parts of a good chipping set-up:

- narrow stance – shot does not require a wide base
- ball positioned opposite right, big toe
- weight roughly 60% on left leg
- hands a couple of inches down the handle for control
- hands in front of lap, creating shaft lean towards target

The Chipping Motion

The chipping motion resembles the putting motion with the swinging of the club controlled by the arms and shoulders. The wrists remain stable with absolutely no cupping or scooping through impact. As with the full swing, your job is to achieve solid contact by swinging down through the ball, letting the loft of the club do the job of getting the ball into the air.

Pitching

The pitch is generally played when you are farther from the green. It is a shot that flies higher, and typically spends more than half of its time in the air. Like chipping, your job is to strike down through the ball and let the loft of the wedge dictate the height of the shot.

The Set-Up

The set-up for the pitch is similar to the chip with a couple of small adjustments.

- The longer the distance the wider the stance becomes.
- The ball is typically located more forward in the stance, approaching the middle but still slightly back of centre.
- Roughly 60% of your weight is on your left foot.
- Hands, as always, remain in front of lap.

The Pitching Motion

The pitching motion resembles a small swing. Because the ball will be travelling higher and farther through the air, the motion must be longer and produce more clubhead speed than for a chip. To produce the longer swing, wrist hinge and more arm swing are required. The length of the swing will be dictated by the length of the shot, and control over distance will need to be developed with practice. The motion should create a downward blow through the ball, with the club contacting the ground just after impact.

Partial Wedge Shots

Partial wedge shots range from 25 to 75 yards, depending on how far you hit your full wedge shots.

The Set-Up

The set-up for these shots is similar to the pitch with a couple of small adjustments.

- The longer the distance the wider the stance
- The ball is typically located more in the middle of the stance because the motion is more like a full swing.
- Roughly 60% of your weight is on your left foot.
- Hands, as always, are in front of lap

The Motion

The partial wedge technique is very similar to the pitch with the length of the swing being dictated by the required distance of the shot. Solid contact is achieved with a downward blow creating a small and shallow divot just after impact. I advocate a system that uses three different swings for each of your wedges and gives you several repeatable yardages. Most golfers find three lengths of swings comfortable. As the photos on the next page show, I label the swings by the location of my left arm relative to the face of a clock, at the end of the backswing. The length of backswing and follow through should be roughly the same. It is okay for the follow through to be a little longer than the backswing, but to ensure an accelerating motion through the ball, it is <u>not</u> desirable for the backswing to be longer than the follow through.

With a little practice, you will find you can get quite good with these three swings. The system will give you three comfortable yardages for each wedge in your bag and will let you handle many more situations with success. I carry four wedges, so this system gives me twelve yardages to work with from 30 to 120 yards. As a result, I rarely face a shot that is an uncomfortable yardage. In a short period of time, you can take a part of the game that scares most average golfers and turn it into a strength.

Imagine how much fun golf will be when you are excited to hit a 50-yard shot over a bunker, because you know it is one of the shots you have practiced and have confidence playing.

7:30 Wedge Swing

9:00 Wedge Swing

10:30 Wedge Swing

The Sand Shot

The sand shot is played differently than the other scoring shots and requires some adjustments to the set-up and swing. The technique is learned with two main goals in mind, to control both HOW and WHERE the clubhead enters the sand.

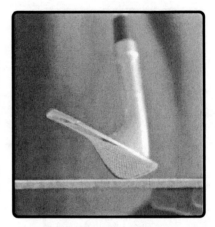

First, the how. Ideally, the sand shot is played with the wedge gliding through the sand with relatively little friction. This gliding is promoted by the bounce of the club. Bounce is the feature that positions the back edge of the sole lower than the leading edge and keeps the leading edge from digging into the sand. This digging causes the club to slow down quickly and creates problems with distance control. I will focus on the actual technique used to create the ideal contact in a moment.

> *Bounce is a feature that locates the back edge of the sole lower than the leading edge.*

Now, the where. You have undoubtedly experienced the breathtaking beauty of a sand shot struck without any sand, as it soars over the green and out of sight. You have probably also enjoyed the jar to your entire body caused by hitting way too far behind the ball, and the convenience of getting to play your next shot from right there in front of you. The ultimate reason for both of these score wreckers is that you haven't learned to control where the club enters the sand. Let's work on getting rid of this problem.

The Set-Up

The set-up for the sand shot is designed to promote the desired contact point with the sand and to accentuate the bounce of the club. Some set-up fundamentals to work with:

- Feet are dug into the sand for stability and to test the consistency of the sand.
- *Open stance* promotes body clearance during swing and an outside-in swing.
- Clubface is considerably open to the target with the key being you open the clubface BEFORE you form your grip. The open clubface increases the bounce of the club, further helping the club glide through the sand.
- Ball is positioned towards the front of your stance.
- Butt of club is pointing towards the middle of your body, positioning handle behind the ball. This also increases the bounce of the club.
- Your weight is evenly distributed.

Sand Set-Up

The Sand Motion

The motion is different than for most other shots in that you don't close the clubface as you swing through the ball, you hold the clubface open. The clubface should face the sky as it swings through impact to ensure the leading edge doesn't contact the sand first.

The backswing should be more vertical than the other scoring game shots with no lateral body motion to the right. This will help you control the entry point of the clubhead into the sand which, depending on the type of sand, should be between one and two inches behind the ball. A typical problem for a lot of golfers is making their normal full swing with the usual weight shift to the right during the backswing. This lateral motion results in an approach to the ball that is too shallow and often results in a *thin* shot sending the ball much too far.

tip time!

Test the Sand

As you dig your feet into the sand to get better footing, note the firmness of the sand. If the sand is soft and fluffy your club will glide easily through the sand and less power will be needed. If the sand is firm, strike the sand closer to the ball to avoid your club bouncing off the firm surface into the back of the ball.

Level Two - Distance Control

After working on your technique for a while, you will be capable of hitting your short shots with consistent contact. You will then be ready to develop the ability to control how far you shots fly through the air.

Distance control requires learning how much clubhead speed is needed to propel the ball different distances through the air. Simply put, the farther you need the ball to fly, the longer your swing will need to be. Chip shots are played with relatively little wrist hinge in the backswing, but as you move farther from the green, you will need to incorporate wrist action into your swing to increase the length of your backswing and create more clubhead speed. The trick is learning how much clubhead speed you need to carry the ball the desired distance.

Many golfers struggle because they either make too short a backswing and have to accelerate the club abruptly in the forward swing, or they make a backswing that is too long for the required shot and need to decelerate as they approach impact to avoid hitting the ball too far. Both of these scenarios lead to major problems with contact and distance control.

Some people find it helpful to imagine an underhand tossing motion when they are learning the smooth rhythm of the scoring shots. The arm should swing back and through without any jerky movements. This is the motion required to successfully hit chips and pitches.

Many golfers encounter problems when they get too far from the green to hit a basic pitch and are still too close for a full wedge shot. These partial wedge shots require a lot of practice to become proficient. The three swing system on page 91 will help make these shots easier to learn and execute on the course. Working with the three swings will give you three comfortable yardages with each wedge in your bag, and will give you many more options to handle those shots from 30 to 90 yards.

Learning distance control out of the sand is another project, because you will need a much more powerful swing than normal to hit the ball a certain distance. Developing a feel for how the sand will affect the speed of the club and the resulting distance of the shot will take some practice. Like the rest of the scoring game, learning this feel will only be possible when you are able to make consistent contact.

Level Three - Controlling the Amount of Roll

There are three ways to control roll. The easiest way is to control the trajectory or height of your shots. The higher the ball flies, the less it will roll when it lands. The other ways to limit how far the ball rolls are by landing the ball in longer grass or into an upslope, or by putting extra backspin on the shot.

Trajectory Control

Controlling trajectory is accomplished by learning to use the appropriate loft. Loft is controlled by three factors: the club you select, the angle of the shaft at impact, and the squareness of the clubface at impact. You can create lower shots by selecting a less lofted club to hit the shot, or by playing the ball back in your stance causing the shaft of the club to lean more towards the target, thereby, decreasing the effective loft of the club. Every degree the shaft leans towards or away from the target will either decrease or increase the loft of the club.

You can hit the ball higher by selecting a club with more loft, playing the ball more forward in your stance, and/or opening the clubface.

To give your scoring game a good foundation, find one ball position that allows you to learn solid contact and learn the trajectory caused by each of your clubs. Practice is required to learn how far each of your clubs will roll after landing, but the chart to the right will give you a general guideline to help you begin the process. Once you can control one set-up position, experiment with the various ways to alter your shots' trajectory.

Eventually you will find your most lofted club doesn't hit the ball as high as you need for certain situations. When this happens more advanced golfers can "build a new club" by changing how their most lofted club sits at set-up and arrives at impact.

Approximate Flight to Roll Ratios		
SW	--	1 : 1
PW	--	1 : 2
9I	--	1 : 3
8I	--	1 : 4
7I	--	1 : 5
6I	--	1 : 6

There are two ways of adding loft to a club, opening the clubface, and leaning the shaft away from the target by moving the ball forward in your stance. Below are some pictures of a high lob shot. Notice the ball position is forward in my stance, the clubface is open at set-up, and when I make the swing, I slide the club under the ball, sending it up quickly.

The High Lob Shot

> *The lob shot requires cushion under the ball so you can open the clubface and then slide the club under the ball during the forward swing. You will need a long swing to hit the ball a short distance.*

A note of caution about the lob shot. When you open the clubface substantially to hit a high lob, it increases the amount of bounce on the club. Increasing bounce will cause the leading edge of the club to sit higher off the ground and more cushion will be needed under the ball to avoid the wedge bouncing off the gound and into the ball. These techniques also create risk, because you will need to make a relatively big swing to propel the ball a short distance. The bigger swing can result in a dramatically long shot if you strike the ball with the leading edge of the club rather than sliding the clubface under the ball. This shot requires precision and commitment, so you should practice it many times before trying it on the course. Learning to hit the ball high is an easy way to make the ball stop quickly and will give you the ability to handle challenging shots over bunkers or to hole locations near the edge of the green.

Other Ways to Stop Your Ball

Another way to stop a shot is to land the ball in longer grass or into an upslope. This type of shot comes with some uncertainty, as the ball is likely to bounce unpredictably and might roll the wrong distance or direction. Landing a shot in longer grass is a good alternative if you aren't comfortable with hitting the high shot, or if your lie doesn't provide enough cushion under the ball to play the higher shot.

Backspin

I am always asked how to hit those little shots that land, take two bounces, and then stop dead like the pros hit on TV. As I stated earlier in the chapter, beginner and intermediate players should learn one basic technique to consistently control contact, trajectory, and roll before attempting any type of advanced shot.

All shots hit with lofted clubs have backspin. Creating enough spin on your scoring shots to make them stop quickly requires a few things. You need a clean lie on a firm surface, and you need to hit the ball solidly with a descending blow, "pinching" it against the ground. This causes it to spin up the clubface a little more quickly. Clean grooves on the clubface will help, and finally, you need the courage to try the shot.

This shot should be practiced extensively before being tried on the course. Most golfers should work on mastering the basic shots before trying to learn this shot. For this reason, in the section on shot selection, I focus on using trajectory to control roll because it is more relevant to most golfers. If you desperately want to use the spinner, spend time to learn the shot and how it reacts after it lands and factor that amount of roll into your landing zone selection. Remember, the pros on TV spend hours polishing their short games so, if you can't spend a lot of time practicing, be realistic with your shot selections.

Choosing the Correct Shot

People are always asking me; "When should I chip and when should I pitch?" In my world these are just words, and they only confuse the issue. My answer is simple; "You should use a long enough swing to fly the ball the distance you need". Spend time learning the relationship between clubhead speed and distance and then use the length of swing that fits the situation. I prefer you not get bogged down by trying to decide which shot to use.

Before you prepare to play any scoring shot, you need to answer two questions: Where are you going to land the shot, and what trajectory do you need so that after the ball lands, it will roll to the hole?

Whenever possible, try to land your shots about five feet onto the putting surface and let the ball roll to the hole. Landing the ball in this zone will be beneficial for a few reasons:

- Landing the ball on the green will make the first bounce easier to judge.

- Trying to land the ball five feet onto the green will give you some clearance from the fringe, if you don't quite reach your landing zone.

- Picking a spot on the green, close to you will let you use the shortest possible swing. This is positive because your chances of getting solid contact are better with a shorter swing and a miss-hit will be less punishing.

- By always considering the five foot rule first, you can often come to a quick decision on shot selection, eliminating doubt and second guessing.

tip time!

Whenever possible, land your ball about five feet onto the green and let it roll to the hole.

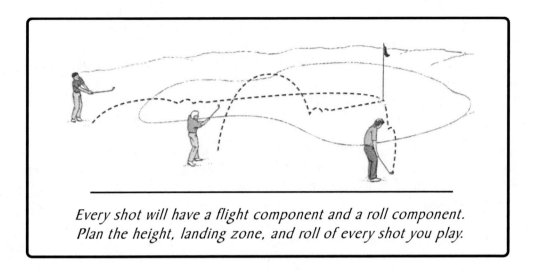

Every shot will have a flight component and a roll component.
Plan the height, landing zone, and roll of every shot you play.

There are three criteria that will determine whether you can use the five feet onto the green guideline when choosing your shot.

1. Is the landing zone relatively flat so judging the bounce will be easy?   If it is sloped, move your spot to a point five feet onto a flatter area.

2. Will the lie allow you to play the type of shot needed for you to land the ball in your zone? For example, if your ball is sitting poorly, and landing the ball five feet onto the green would require a high lob shot, you will need to move your landing zone. In every case, the shot selection needs to have a landing zone and a desired trajectory for the appropriate amount of roll. The shot selection needs to be consistent with what your lie will allow you to do.

3. Will your present skill level allow you to successfully execute the shot? If the answer is 'no', you will have to relocate your landing zone and shot requirements to fit your skills.

When assessing a situation, visualize the shot that would be necessary if you were to land the ball five feet onto the surface. If this shot is within your skill level and the lie will allow you to hit it, select the club needed and play the shot. If your skill or the lie makes that shot too risky, pick a shot you can successfully pull off. Select the landing zone that will work with the anticipated amount of roll on the shot you have selected. If the only available landing zone will result in the ball rolling too far or too short, take your lumps and try to make a long putt.

You will encounter a number of different lies, ranging from long rough to hard, baked-out turf. There is no substitute for experimentation when it comes to your short game. Spend as much time as you can, hitting shots from all kinds of situations during practice, so you are better prepared to handle them on the course. For instruction on these shots you can learn more in an hour with a teaching pro than I can teach you here, with a hundred pages. Profesionals have spent hours working on the scoring game and can pass on their secrets

When you find yourself in a challenging and defensive position, play a conservative shot, and try to get the ball onto the middle of the green. Many golfers rack up high scores by trying to get cute with difficult shots and end up adding a couple of extra strokes to their score in the process.

Here are some basic suggestions for tricky shots:

Long Rough

Since solid contact is impossible with long grass around your ball, play it like a bunker shot. Open the club face and make a bigger swing than normally needed for the required distance. Through impact, try to slide the club under the ball. The clubface will tend to close down when it enters the grass, so make a special effort to keep the clubface open through the hitting zone. Practice will help you learn to judge the rough's effects on distance.

Hard Turf

The most dangerous part of this shot is the likelihood the club will bounce off the ground and *skull* the ball, if you don't hit the ball first. To avoid this, play the ball further back in you stance than normal. This will promote an exaggerated descending blow into the ball, ensuring clean contact. Because you have decreased the loft of your club, take this into account when selecting a club or allowing for roll.

Buried Lie in a Bunker

When your ball is buried in a bunker, conventional sand technique will result in the ball coming out low and rolling a long way. To hit a higher and softer shot from a buried lie, make a very upright backswing using only your wrists and arms. On the downswing, accelerate the clubhead abruptly into the sand, just behind the ball. As the photo shows, the shot requires virtually no follow through. The sand will blast up and forward, carrying the ball out with less forward momentum than the conventional sand technique would create.

Practicing Your Scoring Game

You will find a scoring game assessment form in Appendix C. As with your putting, this will give you an excellent tool for assessing your present skills, and make it fun for you to keep track of your improvement.
Complete control of contact is the vital first step, so this is where your practice should begin. If you are worried about sculling or *chunking* your shots you have very little chance of successfully executing a shot. Start with chipping from right next to the green and move into the longer pitch shots as your performance improves.

When your pitching motion becomes repeatable, you are ready to venture into the sand. Your initial practice in the sand should focus on making swings that result in the back edge of the sole entering the sand first. When this becomes second nature, you can start getting more picky about where the clubhead enters the sand. Work towards striking the sand at the exact point you have picked. When you feel confident in this ability, add a golf ball by placing it roughly two inches in front of the point where your divots have been starting. Your goal will be to continue making divots which start a couple of inches before the ball.

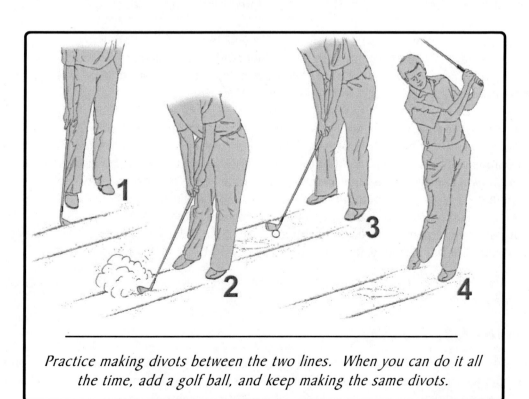

Practice making divots between the two lines. When you can do it all the time, add a golf ball, and keep making the same divots.

When your technique is sound, and contact is consistently good, switch your focus to flying the ball different distances. Distance control is entirely learned, so you may find it difficult at first. It is important for your contact to remain consistent when you are focusing on distance. If you find your contact becomes inconsistent when you change your focus, go back to level one and solidify your technique. If your contact remains good when you introduce a distance target, you're on your way to developing a good scoring game.

To develop your distance control, spread balls all over your practice area, and work on landing the balls on the same spot from various locations. I typically put a tee in the ground to signify my landing zone, and try to land all of my balls near the tee.

When you can land your shots near your target zone with regularity, you can then move on to level three, roll control. To begin the process, use a couple of clubs which differ greatly in loft, such as a pitching wedge and 7-iron. From the same spot and using the same landing zone, hit several shots with each club. You will notice the 7-iron shots roll considerably further than the pitching wedge. Remember the flight to roll ratios from page 109, and see if your numbers are similar. When you are comfortable with these two clubs, you can start using all of your clubs for the short shots to create different amounts of roll.

Some golfers find it productive to actually pace the distance from their ball to the hole, and then calculate the flight to roll ratio for each shot so they can select the right club. If your mind works this way and you can do it without holding up play, go ahead. Most golfers simply develop the knack for picking the right club for the situation.

I can usually narrow my selection to two possible clubs and then make my final decision based on the shot at hand. For example, if I have narrowed my choice to my pitching wedge and 9-iron, I will assess the speed of the green, the slope between my ball and the hole, and from which side of the hole I would rather putt. If the greens are very fast, if I am chipping downhill, or, if I would rather putt from the short side of the hole, I would select the more lofted pitching wedge to decrease the chances of the ball rolling too far. If, on the other hand, the greens are slow, I am chipping uphill, or, I don't mind my ball rolling past the hole a little bit, I would select the less lofted 9-iron to promote a little more roll.

After a little bit of practice you should always be able to narrow your options to two clubs and then make your decision based on the situation.

Practice Like You Play

Use a short game test like the one in Appendix C to assess your short game needs and chronicle your improvement. The test won't take long. It will put you under a little bit of pressure and let you evaluate your performance accurately.

To really improve your short game make every shot during practice, as close to game conditions as possible by using the following ideas:

- Play the ball as it sits, regardless of the lie. Practicing recovery shots from poor lies will prepare you for the inevitable bad luck on the course.

- Hit each shot to a different target or from a different distances. Varying your shots will teach you to select the right shot for each situation.

- Hit a shot and then go putt it in the hole. This is the ultimate way to practice your short game. Keep score and see how many times out of ten you can get up and down in two shots.

- Experiment with different clubs and different techniques. You can never have too many shots around the greens.

There is no substitute for practice where your scoring game is concerned. Learn good technique, and then spend every available moment learning the shots that will let you get the ball close to the hole from various lies. I promise you, a good scoring game will give you that elusive consistency in scoring, almost every golfer dreams about.

Chapter Summary

- The scoring game has three levels:
  1. Consistent contact
  2. Distance control
  3. Roll control

- You will always struggle until you get control over contact.

- Spend many hours practicing your scoring game.

Many golfers struggle to perform on the course because of a poor mental game. Practicing the mental game will help remove mental interference and turn your brain into a valuable tool rather than an obstacle to overcome.

Chapter Nine
The Mental Game

The mental game is comprised of several skills, or traits, that you need to develop so your physical potential can be reached on a consistent basis. Your performance on any given day is determined by your talent level, minus the effects of mental interference, and plus or minus the effects of luck. You are not in control of luck, although, some would say luck is the residue of hard work. What you can control is your talent and the quality of your mental skills, which determine the amount of mental interference you encounter while playing.

Your physical skills can be improved and maintained over time with effective practice. I have focused on those areas in other chapters. The mental skills key to your performance are focus, confidence, relaxation, visualization, and emotional stability. Like most skills, you have to learn and maintain them to keep them strong. Mental skills are dependent on each other for successful performance. I will discuss each of them on their own, and then show you how to put them together into a pre-shot routine that will let your talent rise to the surface when you play.

Focus and Concentration

I define focus as the ability to concentrate on the one thing that is most important at any moment in time. It is only possible to concentrate on one thing at a time. For golf, we need to be able to remain focused on the shot we are playing and avoid distractions.

Golfers, who remain completely devoted to the shot at hand and don't fall victim to negative thoughts or other distractions, always play up to their capabilities.

> Your performance on any given day is determined by subtracting the effects of mental interference from your talent level, and then factoring in the effects of luck.

Golf is a game played over 4 hours, but the actual time needed to go through your routine and hit all of the shots is only about 60 minutes. It is virtually impossible to maintain focus for the entire round, so one of your challenges is learning how to move in and out of focus quickly and effectively.

Another challenging part of golf is that there are two kinds of focus needed to play well. You need a wide focus while analyzing the situation and gathering information pertinent to the shot at hand. You must then narrow your focus to the target while playing the shot. To play smart golf you must be aware of the hazards in front of you when selecting a shot, but after the decision has been made, work only with images of the desired shot.

Gather the information affecting your shot, make a plan and then cross the decision line and focus exclusively on the target as you execute the shot.

You have probably had the experience on the course when you were distracted by a mosquito landing on a pond, three fairways over. You may also have had the more desirable experience of hitting a golf shot, after which someone in your group expressed surprise that you didn't back away from the shot because a car had driven by. You didn't back away, because you hadn't even heard it go by. This is the kind of focus you need all the time.

The good news is, the ability to remain focused, is a skill you can learn at home in your easy chair. The following is a good practice drill to help you heighten your focusing abilities and become less susceptible to distraction.

To work on your ability to concentrate, you need a room with both a radio and television. Set the volume levels of both machines to the same level and sit in a comfortable chair facing the TV. Begin by trying to block out the sights and sounds of the TV and focusing only on the radio. Ideally, the radio will be tuned to a talk station to be most distracting. After a couple of minutes, switch your focus to watching and listening to the TV, while completely blocking out the sound of the radio. After two more minutes, switch your focus again to watching the TV while listening to the radio.

The development of the ability to concentrate when potential distractions are present, will make it possible for you to stay committed to the target during your shots and avoid those negative thoughts that pop into your head at exactly the wrong moment.

Staying in the NOW

For optimal performance you will need to remain focused on the process of hitting a good golf shot, and avoid thinking about the perceived consequences attached to the outcome of the shot. Your ability to accurately gather data about the upcoming shot, formulate a plan, and focus on the execution of the shot will greatly increase the chances of hitting a good shot. To consistently hit good golf shots, you cannot be thinking about the past or future, you must be engrossed in the present. This is called staying in the "NOW".

You have probably experienced the effects of letting your mind wander to your final score, rather than focusing on the shot at hand. Have you ever shot a really good front nine score only to follow it up with an especially poor back nine? This was caused by your loss of focus on each shot and becoming too concerned with the end result. You certainly didn't forget how to play golf somewhere between the ninth green and tenth tee! Taking it one shot at a time is a cliché, but it is necessary to play your best golf. If you can learn to approach every shot the same way, with complete attention to the steps needed to hit that one shot, you will avoid the pitfalls of getting ahead of yourself or dwelling on poor shots from earlier in the round.

Allowing your mind to wonder to the final score or consequences of a shot, will sabotage your game every time. Even the world's best golfers have counter-productive thoughts jump into their heads. They quickly recognize them and have strategies to use when they happen. The next time you find your brain looking into the future, stop and recognize that it has happened, then return your attention to the steps needed to successfully hit the next shot. Go through your pre-shot routine, focusing on each step with complete concentration, and hit the shot as you always do.

You will find as you work on your concentration skills at home, you will be less easily distracted and be able to get your focus back to the job at hand much more quickly.

Your ability to remain focused on the details important to the execution of each shot will have a very positive effect on the level of your play, especially when pressure mounts and distractions are more prominent. All of the other mental skills described in this chapter are important, so your ability to stay focused can be mastered.

Learning to stay in the now begins with effective practice. Hitting a large portion of your practice balls in each session, just as you would on the course, will prepare you for actual game performance. There is much more on effective practice in Section Three.

Confidence

The level of confidence you have in a skill is often more important than the actual amount of skill you possess. Thinking you can do something will often cover for a lack of ability. A popular phrase says, "whether you think you can or you can't, you are right". Confidence in yourself is vital to your level of play. Confidence in your own abilities significantly decreases your chance of loosing your focus or becoming distracted by unimportant details.

Your self-image plays a major part in how confident you feel in certain situations. A golfer with a positive self-image will view a poor shot, as an aberration, while a golfer with a lesser view of his or her game, will use a poor shot to put him or herself down even more. The good news is, if you are a person with low "golf esteem", you can get past it.

To build confidence, you must redefine who you are as a golfer. To do this you probably need to change how you look at your golf shots, and more importantly, how you react to them. Your brain remembers things more easily when you attach emotional importance to them. The average golfer reacts to a bad shot with varying degrees of anguish, ranging from a gentle sigh to a loud, self-targeted tongue lashing, questioning his or her right to ever play golf again! What's worse, when most golfers finally hit a good shot they use it to further abuse their psyche, saying things like: "It's about time".

You may need to approach your golf shots differently. You learned earlier that the golf ball tells you, with its flight, exactly what your club was doing at impact. You need to view your poor shots as data for learning and nothing else, and your good shots as something to build on. I'm not asking you to go into Tiger-like, fist-pumping dementia every time you hit the green with a wedge shot, but giving yourself a discreet congratulation afterwards, will go a long way to building your confidence.

To really make this a part of your learning process, I recommend the following procedure. When you are practicing or playing, and hit a poor shot, acknowledge it as a poor shot, identify the swing error you have made, and then immediately make a swing the correct way. After making the correct swing, validate the good swing and move on. If you hit a good shot, validate your result and move on. This way, your poor swings are reacted to with indifference, and after every single shot you are building your database of good images from which to draw. This process will help you feel better about your golf game very quickly.

Another factor, which contributes to your level of confidence, is the quality of your preparation for each round of golf. If you have been practicing frequently, taking care of yourself with a good diet and lots of sleep, and, if you have a good game plan for the course you are playing, you will feel ready, and your confidence will grow.

Another way to improve your golf esteem is to use positive affirmations. Saying statements like "I am a good putter" or "I never give up" to yourself, will help increase your confidence. Many great golfers have posted these kinds of positive phrases on their bathroom mirrors or fridges so they would see them and repeat them several times each day.

One last way to build confidence is to act like you are confident. Fake it, until you make it. By acting confident and walking with a sense of purpose, you will start to feel more self-assured. You can trick yourself into being confident by acting like someone who is confident!

Relaxation

I don't know about you, but when I get tense and my muscles tighten up, I don't play my best golf! If you can remain calm and relaxed, you give yourself a much better chance to succeed. In this day and age, you may be tense all the time and not even know it. Controlling your tension levels will allow for optimal performance by reducing tension in your muscles, and eliminate the chance of having your focus interrupted by physical discomfort or tension when you are faced with an important shot.

Muscle tension is one of the biggest enemies of golfers. A tight body, especially through the shoulders, arms and hands, causes your swing to become shorter and faster.

This can inhibit your ability to consistently square the clubface, and usually destroys your rhythm and timing. Furthermore, being in a relaxed state makes it possible for you to use the other mental skills discussed in this chapter. There are many books written exclusively about relaxation, so I will not attempt to give you a lengthy rundown on all of the various methods. I would like to make you aware of the importance of avoiding tension, and give you some basic concepts with which to work. It is important that you find a relaxation system that works for you, and practice it often, so it is a skill you can call on when needed.

The first step in combating tension is learning to recognize when you are becoming tense. You can learn to identify your own symptoms, but here are some of the more common signs of increased tension or anxiety:

- raised shoulders
- jaw clinched and pushed forward.
- shallow breathing
- feeling of coldness in hands and feet
- squinting eyes

You must first recognize the symptoms, so you can use your relaxation skills to ease them. Eventually you can learn to remain calm most of the time by building some relaxation techniques into your regular routine. For example, I typically get quite tight through the shoulders when I get nervous and my breathing gets shallow. To combat this, I take a couple of deep breaths and shrug my shoulders a couple of times during my pre-shot routine in an effort to remain relaxed.

To help combat tension around my eyes, I play golf in sunglasses most of the time. Okay, it's partly because it looks cool, but it's amazing how much more relaxed I feel after a round when I have worn sunglasses. Try this experiment: squint your eyes like you are looking into the sun and hold that position for 30 seconds. You can't help but feel tense. Notice how much more relaxed you feel, after you relax your eyes and face. Sunglasses are also very important to protect your eyes from the harmful effects of the sun.

A very common approach to relaxation is the systematic tensing and relaxing of the different muscle groups in your body. At first, you should practice this approach in a dimly lit room with some soft music playing. While sitting comfortably in a chair, start by tensing your feet for a few seconds and then relaxing them, feeling the tension flow out of your feet. Next, do the same for your legs, stomach, chest, shoulders, neck, arms, and hands. You will feel the tension slowly leaving your body as you work your way up your body. It may take you a while to relax your whole body initially, but with practice you will be able to develop the skill and attain a relaxed condition in only a couple of minutes.

By practicing this skill you will become much more aware of your body's tension levels and be better equipped to maintain a more relaxed state while playing. You may find this technique helps you sleep better as well!

Visualization

Seeing is believing. Your ability to "see" yourself making a good swing or silky smooth putting stroke before you hit a shot will greatly increase your success rate. Visualization can be a very powerful tool, but, for most golfers it works against them. How many times have you come to a difficult hole, noticed the trouble on the right side and seen an image of your ball flying to the right and into the trouble? Where does your ball normally go after this happens?

Many golfers make the mistake of focusing on where they don't want to hit their ball rather than where they want it to go. When you are driving your car, are you looking in the ditch or down the road? I hope you said down the road! Your brain doesn't understand words like "don't", it works with images. If you tell yourself "don't hit it to the right", all that registers in your brain is "hit it to the right", and you get a nice clear image of a shot going to the right. To illustrate this point, close your eyes and tell yourself not to think of a big banana split. I'm willing to bet my lunch money, you had an image of an ice cream treat bounce into your head! Visualization is a powerful tool and you need to be using it to your advantage.

Many pros, when asked what they think about before an important shot, respond that they remember the best shot they have ever hit with that particular club, and then try to hit it again. This is awesome in its simplicity. What do most golfers do? Have a flash back of some awful shot they have hit before, and proceed to hit the same shot again.

You need to learn how to positively visualize the outcome of each shot so you can stop sabotaging your golf swing. As I stated earlier in the chapter, your golf esteem will play a large role in determining the kinds of images that jump into your head. You can learn to control what your mind sees.

The skill of positively visualizing the outcome before you swing, needs to be learned and continuously practiced. Much like relaxation, the best place to start is in a quiet place somewhere at home. Start out simple and visualize yourself successfully making a two-foot putt. When you can "see" yourself make a number of putts without an interruption in the flow of the images, you can slowly expand your visualizations. Before too long, you should be able to visualize an entire swing. Eventually, you want to get to the point where you can watch the whole swing and then the entire flight of the ball until it lands, and rolls into the hole. This will take a while, but the more you practice, the better you will become.

This skill will be very valuable in both your pre-shot routine that we will discuss in a moment and when we look at learning new skills in Chapter Thirteen. Seeing yourself hitting a good shot or making a good motion is very helpful to your performance. Studies have shown that your brain doesn't distinguish between vividly imagined motions and those actually completed.

Emotional Stability

I refer to emotional stability in golf, as the ability to remain within the optimal range of arousal for high performance. Controlling fear, anger, and your level of relaxation are necessary skills.

It sounds crazy, but the game of golf can strike fear in the hearts of even the most tour-tested professionals. Letting your thoughts shift to what people will think about your play, or placing too much importance on a certain shot can illicit fear and anxiety. Dealing with your anger productively is also very important. Most competitive people feel anger or frustration when the game is not going according to plan. How you deal with this emotion is critical to your level of play.

Anger is a state of arousal. The keys to good anger management on the course are using the energy to become more focused on the task at hand, without letting your anger cause foolish decisions about course management. Anger causes you to become tense and releases hormones into your systems that spike your adrenaline. This, almost always decreases your effectiveness.

Finally, you should remain on a steady emotional level. Avoid allowing yourself to get too high when things are going well or too low when you are struggling.

Your job is to remain within your personal arousal range for optimal performance. Some golfers need to work on increasing their arousal levels. They are almost too relaxed or emotionally uninterested. Most golfers, especially when angered, need to manage their arousal to avoid becoming too agitated to execute a good swing. It is far better to release anger outwardly, as opposed to sending it deep inside. This requires a socially acceptable way to dispose of the excess energy. Many professionals, who are under constant scrutiny, use discreet, but outward vents for the anger. They train themselves to feel less angry when they do things like loosening the Velcro on their glove or hiking up their pants. This would require you to spend some time *"anchoring"* a movement to cause a certain physiological response when needed. This procedure falls outside my area of expertise, but you can find books on the subject, or enlist the help of a sports psychologist, if this is a major concern.

Building a Pre – Shot Routine

One of the biggest frustrations for most golfers is their inability to perform on the course as well as they do during practice. The average golfer doesn't practice the skills needed to cope with the pressures of the golf course. One of the most important tools you need, to become a consistent golfer, is a solid "Pre-Shot Routine".

A pre–shot routine, much as it sounds, is a series of steps good golfers go through EVERY time they play a golf shot. If you truly want to start performing up to your capabilities on the course, you need to build a rock solid routine. You then need to use it on every shot you hit on the course, as well as a large percentage of your shots during practice.

Golfers' routines vary and should be personalized depending on your personality. Here are some suggestions based on common characteristics included in most good routines and the order in which they generally happen.

- Data gathering - Spend time assessing how the ball is sitting, where your target should be, based on your skill level, the distance to that target, wind conditions, and anything else that will potentially affect your shot.

- Relaxation - Take a couple of deep breaths to help relax your muscles and focus your mind.

- Visualization - From a position behind your ball and facing your target, "see" the shot you are about to hit. This is a skill which needs to be learned and the better you get at seeing the exact shot you would like to hit, the better your shots will become. Your target should also be as precise as possible. It is a proven fact that your body performs better when your brain gives it very precise instructions. Take darts for example; even novice dart players will rarely miss the entire board if it is their intent to hit the bull's eye. In golf, rather than trying to hit the fairway, aim for a specific tree or flag stick in the distance. Even if your golf swing rarely sends the ball in the direction you have chosen, if you pick a smaller target your poor shots will be more manageable.

- Rehearsal - Make a practice swing "feeling" the speed and motion required to hit your desired shot. From this point forward, you must remain focussed on the target and avoid thoughts about your swing mechanics or the importance of the shot. When you approach the ball, you step across the "decision line" and need to enter execution mode.

⏸ Set-Up - Go through your steps for setting up. Place your hands on the club, position your body to the ball, achieve good posture, and ensure good alignment.

⏸ Trigger - When you are finished your set-up procedure, give yourself the go ahead to swing. Most good swings begin with a "trigger", like a slight forward press or tweak of a knee. You may find it easier to initiate your swing with a small movement to get you going.

If, at any time during your routine, you encounter negative thoughts, you should abort and begin again. At first, you may find it hard to get all the way through an entire routine without any bad thoughts. This is why you will probably need to practice this skill on the practice tee. Your ability to go through your routine every time and without negative thoughts will let you play up to your physical abilities every time you play.

Pre-Shot Routine

1. Make a plan and visualize the shot.
2. Rehearse the swing.
3. Set-up to the ball.
4. Check your target.
5. Use a trigger to start swing.

Chapter Summary

- Good mental skills will allow your talent to be fully utilized.

- To be the best you can be you need to maintain your focus.

- To remain focussed, you must avoid distractions caused by lack of confidence, muscle tension or allowing your mind to wander to the past or future.

- A pre-shot routine will be a valuable tool for helping you remain focused and staying in the now.

Good course management is reliant on your ability to choose the shot you "can" hit, not the shot you "should" be able to hit.

Chapter Ten
Course Management

I define course management as the art of navigating your ball around a golf course. Golf is like pool, in that every shot should be played with the next shot or two in mind, and with the main goal being a good "leave". The tee shot should be played to an area, which provides the best shot to the green. The approach shot to the green should be played to a point that sets up the easiest putt, and even the first putt should be stroked so if it misses, an easy second putt remains. If you were a machine and always hit the ball the distance and direction you wanted to, the game would be easy. Fortunately, we are not perfect and need to consider a few variables when we play our shots.

The biggest key to managing your golf game and producing good scores is knowing your game. Having a clear understanding of what you can and cannot do with your ball is critical to making good decisions regarding each shot.

Some important things to know about your game:

- How far does each of your clubs hit the ball on average?
- What parts of your game are strong and can be relied upon?
- What parts of your game are weak and should be avoided?

The above information will make course management an easy skill to learn.

How Far Do Your Clubs Really Hit It – Be Honest!

When I ask average golfers how far they hit certain clubs I generally get three different answers: "I don't know", "roughly 'X' yards", or "'X' yards when I hit it well". To effectively manage your game, you must know how far you regularly hit each club through the air. This distance must be an average distance and not your "Sunday Best". Spend time with your coach or a friend to determine what your average distance is with each of your clubs and your partial wedge shots. To establish your distances, hit ten shots, throw out the two longest and two shortest, and calculate your average distance, using the other six balls. Write these yardages down for easy reference.

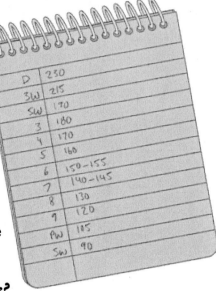

What Are Your Strengths and Weaknesses?

Keeping some statistics about your golf game will give you valuable insight when deciding how to play a golf hole. You must have a clear perspective on your skills to make strategy decisions. Without an inventory of your strengths and weaknesses, you will be left to guess about which shots you should be playing. This will lead to trying shots that aren't within your capabilities. Appendix A is a form I use with my students to help them keep tabs on their games. After only a couple of rounds, you will see some trends in your game. You can then start making changes to your strategy to take advantage of the strong parts of your game, while avoiding the weak parts, until you have a chance to improve them.

What's Your Game Plan?

With a good understanding of your game, you can formulate a plan for how you will play each hole. In a perfect world, you would get a chance to put together your game plan for a certain course the night before you play. The benefit of making a plan before hand, is that the decisions you make, will be realistic and not made in the heat of the battle. Many golfers make the mistake of becoming too aggressive when they start a round poorly, or defensive after a good start to the round. Making decisions about strategy on the fly can compound your errors and make one bad hole turn into two or three. A game plan will give you a blue print for your round, so you can spend more of your on-course time focusing on the execution of shots rather than planning them.

Personal Par

I have my students put together a game plan using their "personal par". Your personal par is the score you would make on a hole, if you played it by hitting a series of average shots for you. If you are a 10-handicapper, your personal par will be a par on the 8 easiest holes on the course, and a bogey on the ten most difficult. You can adjust your par when your game improves, or when you want to challenge yourself.

After setting your personal par, you can plan your strategy for each hole based on the strengths and weaknesses of your game. For example, if your personal par for a long par 4 is a score of 5, your strategy might be to hit a 3-wood off the tee, a middle iron to reach the 100-yard marker, and a wedge onto the green. This strategy would allow you to hit the fairway more often by hitting your 3-wood rather than driver off the tee, play a high percentage second shot with a mid-iron and another high percentage shot onto the green. By playing the percentages and selecting shots well within your capabilities, you would almost always make a five on the hole, and with a good wedge shot or a nice putt you would make your share of par 4's as well.

There are far too many scenarios to run through, but if you take the time to set your personal par for each hole, I think a high percentage strategy will become quite obvious to you.

Choosing the Correct Shot for <u>YOU</u>

Golf is an ever-changing game. Weather conditions and the state of your game are subject to change on a daily or even hourly basis. You may have the best game plan in the history of golf, but you will still face decisions on several of your shots. Picking a target and a desired distance for each of your tee shots is possible in advance, but after that, you need to adapt your plan to wherever your ball decides to go. For each shot, you will need to select a target and a club. Once again, the target you pick should be consistent with your skill level. If you are faced with a long shot over a lake and would have to hit your absolutely best shot to clear the water, you should take a more conservative route to the hole. This may sound like common sense, but you'd be amazed how many golfers try low percentage shots because they think they can pull them off.

Regardless of your skill level, the target you pick should be as precise as possible. You will perform better when the directions your brain gives your body are as specific as possible. Even if you haven't hit the broad side of a barn all day, aiming at a specific tree in the distance, rather than just the fairway, will increase your odds of hitting a good tee shot. In addition, the quality of your poor shots will be raised, which is a key to improved scoring.

Here are three criteria that will help determine if the shot you are considering is a viable option:

1. How are you playing on the day in question?
2. Is the club required to hit the shot one of your stronger clubs or a less reliable one?
3. Are the requirements of the shot within your normal talent range? For example, if the situation requires a high shot that lands softly, are you adept at creating a high trajectory shot with the necessary club?

On a day when you are playing your best and a shot calls for one of your favorite clubs, you are free to try a challenging shot. However, if you are playing poorly you should play the easiest available shot with one of your favorite clubs until your form returns.

The main point I would like you to understand is you need to have a plan for how you intend to play each hole, and your plan must make best use of your current talents.

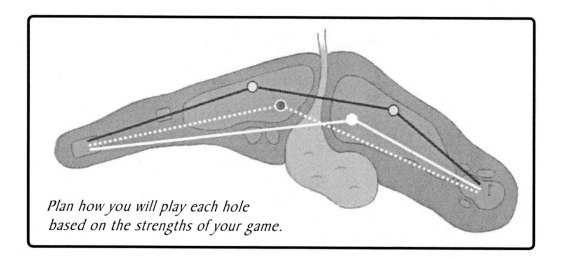

Plan how you will play each hole based on the strengths of your game.

Here a few more things to consider when choosing which shot to play.

The 70% Rule

I advise you to use my 70% Rule. This simply states; if you can't pull off a shot 7 out of 10 times, choose an easier shot. Beginners have trouble with this idea because they can't really hit any shot well 7 out of 10 times. In this situation, you should choose the shot you can play with the highest success rate.

The Middle of the Green Never Moves

Greenskeepers are sometimes very evil. It is widely known, that if they don't get enough sleep, they tend to position the holes very near the edges of greens and, all too often, behind bunkers or water hazards. My advice in situations when you are facing one of these "sucker pins" is to aim at the middle of the green. Don't be tricked into aiming at the pin when it is in a difficult spot. Remember, the middle of the green never moves and you will rarely have a long putt from the center of the green.

Check the Hole Location and Add or Subtract Yardage

The greens on many courses can be upwards of forty or fifty yards long. Most courses now have yardages on the sprinkler heads or markers on the sides of the fairways. It is important to understand these yardages are generally to the middle of the green. In some cases, when the green is fifty yards long, and the hole is located near the back of the green, it may be a full twenty yards back from the center of the green. To choose the correct club, you will need to take the hole location, relative to the middle of the green, into account to calculate your actual distance to the hole. Many golfers leave themselves long putts, after good approach shots, because they fail to add or subtract distance when assessing the situation.

Club Selection in the Wind

Depending on where you live, you may be forced to contend with some strong winds on the course. When playing into or against the wind, the effects are fairly obvious. The helping or hurting effects will depend on the strength of the wind and the height of your shots. Side winds can also affect club selection. If your natural ball flight is curving against a side wind, you will lose distance. If your shot is curving with a side wind, it will fly further. It is always a good idea to play shots close to the ground in high winds, regardless of their direction. The less the wind touches the ball, the less it will affect its flight, and the more control you will have over the shot.

One last thing, when gauging wind speed, tossing grass in the air isn't very helpful. Your ball will be flying a lot higher than your head, so paying attention to what the trees and clouds are doing will give you a much better idea about how the wind might affect your shot. Also, be aware of any large groups of trees that may affect the wind. Situations can arise when you are in an area protected by large trees, but the majority of your ball's flight will be in the open or vice versa. Take note of wind conditions where your ball will be flying, not just where you are standing.

If You Can't Reach the Green - Lay Back

Many golfers make the mistake of always hitting their longest club, even when they can't reach the green. If you can't comfortably reach the green or if there is trouble around the green you want to avoid, try to leave your ball at a distance from the green that will let you play a shot you like. Most golfers have a club or yardage with which they can usually do well. If you can't reach the green, calculate the distance you will need so your next shot is from that preferred yardage, and hit the necessary shot. This strategy will generally make your lay up shot easier and will also increase your chances of hitting it close to the hole on your next shot. I like to call it a 'Lay Back Shot" rather than a "Lay Up Shot", so you will remember to avoid getting too close to a hazard or the green.

Only Take a Risk If the Reward is Worth It

Choosing whether to go for a green from farther out, or hit your driver off a tee, can be a challenging decision. You should only ever choose an aggressive shot if you stand to gain a substantial advantage on the hole <u>and</u> if you are using one of your better clubs.

Before choosing a risky shot, ask yourself if you can realisticly pull the shot off with your skills. Your instincts will let you know, with the feeling you'll get in your gut.

Hit the shortest club possible off the tee that will still leave you a manageable shot into the green. Find the widest portion of the fairway. If you can easily reach the green from that point, hit whatever club you need, to get your ball to that area of the fairway. If you would rather hit your approach from closer in, you need to decide if you would hit the narrower part of the fairway often enough to make the risk worth it.

The only times I personally hit driver off the tee are if I need the added distance to get me to a manageable distance from the green on a par-4, I can potentially drive the green on a par-4, or if I can possibly reach the green in two shots on a par-5 after a long tee shot. If the hole is narrow, or there is substantial risk involved with hitting driver, I will hit a shorter club off the tee and either accept a longer shot to the green, or, in the case of the par-5, accept that I will need three shots to reach the green.

You're probably saying to yourself, yeah, but half the fun of golf is hitting the ball long off the tee. You're absolutely right, but remember the topic at hand is shooting lower scores. If your goal is shooting the lowest score possible, you will take advantage of your strengths and continue to work on your weaknesses during practice. If your goal is to hit long drives, use your driver on every hole and swing as hard as you can, just in case you make contact!!

Would You Rather Go Past the Hole or Come Up Short?

Knowing how far your clubs hit the ball allows you to easily select the appropriate club in most situations. There will be times when you are "in between" clubs and aren't sure which club to choose. There are a couple of ways to deal with this question.

First, determine if you hit better shots when you hit a shot a little harder, or when you swing a little easier. Most golfers fall into one of these two categories.

Secondly, ask yourself, "Would I rather end up short of or past the hole?" If there is trouble short of the green, you should take the longer of the two clubs. If there is trouble behind the hole, you should select the shorter club. Most amateur golfers are chronic under-clubbers, so I would recommend you choose the longer club every time until you consistently hit your shots past the flag.

Know Your Tendencies

This comes with knowing your game. If you are like most golfers, you have a certain shot you tend to hit when you get nervous. Knowing this will let you plan accordingly when you begin feeling anxious. For example, if you tend to lose shots to the right when you get nervous, you will want to choose a club you can easily control and pick targets that give you more room to miss the shot to the right when you are feeling anxious.

When You Get Into Trouble, Get Out In One Shot

Many golfers compound the effects of one bad shot by trying to make a miraculous recovery. If you follow this rule, you will avoid making big numbers. If you are attempting a curving shot or a shot over or under an obstacle, your number one objective is to get your ball past the obstacle and back into play. If you hit the desired shot perfectly and get the ball onto the green, that's great, but you need to avoid getting greedy and hitting the object you are trying to circumnavigate. Remember the 70% Rule for all shots you are going to try.

Listen to Your Little Voice

Golfers often have feelings of uncertainty as they prepare to play a shot. If that little voice inside your head is saying, "Maybe I shouldn't be trying this shot", you need to stop and re-evaluate. After looking at the facts again, you may come to the same decision, but you will have eliminated those nagging doubts. For whatever shot you select, complete commitment will increase your chances of success. That little voice is pretty smart, so you should definitely listen to it!

Avoid the Skull and Crossbones

I use the term "skull and crossbones" to describe areas of the golf course where you just can't hit your ball. On most holes, there will be one side where you can play towards the geen from the trees or rough. On the other side, you will either lose your ball or be unable to reach the green because of trees or other obstacles. That is the skull and crossbones side. In these cases, choose a target that favours the safe side of the hole.

On many occasions, the skull and crossbones will be on the side of the hole which offers a positional advantage for the next shot. Before you choose to go down the dangerous side of the hole, it must fit your level of play that day and call for a shot with one of your more reliable clubs.

Tee Off on the Correct Side of the Tee Box

Many golfers make the mistake of teeing up on the wrong side of the tee box for their normal ball flight. For example, many right-handed slicers tee up on the extreme left hand side of the markers. This seriously decreases their margin for error. By setting up on the extreme right hand side of the tee box, you will have much more room for your slice. If you aren't familiar with this idea, have a pro in your area explain it to you, or you can just take my word for it! Remember, always tee off on the same side of the tee as where your shots tend to miss the fairway.

You Need a "Pet Shot"

All players need a "pet shot". A pet shot is one you can pull off, even under the most pressing of circumstances. To play well under pressure, you need a ball flight that is reliable. It doesn't have to be pretty or exactly the same all the time, but it must curve in the same direction every time.

Most tour professionals have one shot, either a *fade* or a *draw*, they hit on almost every occasion. It may curve 5 yards one time and 20 yards the next, but it never curves the opposite way of what they are trying. This allows them to "eliminate half of the golf course", meaning they don't have to worry about the trouble on one side of the fairway or green.

For example, if their pet shot is a fade and they are a right-handed golfer, they can aim down the left side of the fairway and play their normal shot. If the shot fades 10 yards, it is perfect, if it fades 20 yards, it will be on the right side of the fairway and even if it fades 30 yards, they will only be in the right rough, still able to approach the green. Knowing they will not hit a draw to the left allows them to aim down the left side of the fairway and swing with confidence, because they have a much greater margin for error.

You Also Need a Killer Short Game

The ability to get the ball close to the hole from around the green, and one putt, will allow you to make good decisions from the fairway. Knowing you are a good chipper and putter will permit you to aim at the wide side of greens or play short of the green when there is trouble beside or behind the green. A good short game will also let you fire at pins when you are playing well, because you will have confidence in your ability to get up and down if you miss the green. A good short game will ease the pressure on your long game and allow you to make good decisions.

The First Tee

The tee shot on the first hole, like all challenging shots, puts your swing and mental skills to the test. The pressure you place on yourself to perform, make images of poor shots dance in your head, and tension can take over your muscles. In these situations it is very important for you to select a club you are fond of and play your pet shot. A favourite club and images of a shot you have hit successfully many times will greatly increase your odds of hitting a good shot under pressure.

Chapter Summary

To be a good course manager you need to:

- Know your own game.

- Have a game plan.

- Play within yourself by choosing shots you are capable of hitting.

- Get out of trouble in one shot.

There are many skills in golf, which need to be developed over time. To speed the process, spend plenty of time experimenting during practice.

Chapter Eleven
Special Skills

Special skills is a broad category that I use for everything that doesn't fit into one of the other categories, or, for skills that are learned over time through experience. In this chapter, I will focus on specialty shots to handle many situations, bad weather golf, and playing in competition.

Side Hill Lies

These are the shots you face on a regular basis because most golf courses aren't perfectly flat. To successfully handle hitting shots off sloping ground, you need to make a few adjustments:

- Adapt your set-up position to fit the slope.
- Maintain your body angles and balance during the swing.
- Use a 3/4 swing to promote balance and solid contact.
- Understand the effects of the lie on your ball flight.
- Choose the correct club and aiming point for the shot.
- Play a defensive shot to ensure your next shot will be played from a better lie.

Ball Above Your Feet

When the ball is above your feet, you should grip down on the handle because the ball is closer to you. Set your knee bend and spine angle to sole the club behind the ball. Position your body weight more towards the balls of your feet to avoid losing your balance down the hill. The slope will promote a shot that starts left and hooks, so aim to the right of your target.

Make a shorter, smoother swing to promote good contact and maintain the knee flex and spine tilt you established at set-up.

Ball Below Your Feet

With a ball below your feet, the ball is further away from you. To overcome this challenge, you will need to lower yourself to the ball by tilting more at your hips and increasing the bend in your knees. After adjusting your body angles to get the club behind the ball, position more weight than usual on your heels to help maintain your balance. The slope will promote a fade, so align yourself to the left of your intended target.

Make a shorter, smoother swing to promote good contact and maintain the knee flex and spine tilt you established at set-up.

Downhill Lie

With a downhill lie, you need to move the ball back in your stance, because the slope causes your club to strike the ground earlier in the forward swing. You should set up with your shoulders level to the slope, as in the picture, so your swing will be working with the slope. By tilting your upper body this way, you de-loft the club, causing a lower and longer golf shot. Keep this in mind when choosing which club to use and where your landing spot will be.

Once again, a shorter swing will allow you to stay balanced and make it easier to get clean contact. The tendency is to slide past the ball, resulting in an open clubface at impact, so allow for a fade when you align yourself. You can help avoid this by making a special effort to keep your weight centred between your feet until after contact.

Uphill Lie

Like the downhill lie, you will want to build your set-up position to match the slope by tilting your shoulders to work with the angle of the ground. This lie will add loft to your club leading to a higher and shorter golf shot, so factor this in when you select a club.

The tendency on these shots is to get stuck with your weight on the back foot during the forward swing allowing the club to close too early through impact. To hit your target you will need to either allow for a hook when you align yourself, or better players can attempt to delay the closing of the clubface through impact. As with all side-hill lies, a compact, smooth swing will promote balance and good contact.

Shot Making

Shot making is the ability to control the height and curvature of your shots. Understanding the ball flight laws described on page 17 will make it easier to learn how to make balls curve on purpose. We can all make balls curve; we just want to be able to control when and how much it curves! Being able to intentionally hit the ball low or high and make it curve will allow you to get out of trouble more easily and maximize your scoring ability by avoiding trouble spots in the first place. Creating different ball flights is attainable when you have a repeating golf swing. It will be accomplished primarily with changes to your set-up position. More exaggerated shots will require subtle changes to your swing.

Curving Shots

Curving shots can be created by using the pre-shot adjustments of aiming the clubface where you want the ball to finish, and aligning your body parallel to the direction you want your shot to start. Your body alignment will promote the desired swing path, and the open or closed clubface at set-up will create the desired curvature on your shot. After making the adjustments to your set-up position, you can make your normal swing and the pre-shot geometry will do the rest. This formula assumes you can swing the club parallel to your body alignment and return your hands to square at impact.

Spend considerable time working on these shots so you can learn how much you will need to change your clubface aim and body alignment to create the desired ball flight. I advise you to work on one ball flight until you can consistently control it before you begin trying to learn how to hit a variety of shots.

To intentionally curve shots, aim the clubface where you want the ball to finish and align your body parallel to the direction you want your shot to start.

Trajectory Control

Controlling the height of your shots will make it easier to play in the wind, and let you hit your ball under or over obstacles. Trajectory control is accomplished by controlling the loft of your club at impact. The more loft a club has; the higher the ball will fly. The easiest way to control loft is to choose the appropriate club. Sometimes you will need to hit your clubs higher or lower than normal to satisfy the requirements of a certain situation.

The most important concept to understand for trajectory control is that shaft angle and loft are related. When you take a 5-iron that has roughly 26 degrees of loft and tilt the shaft 5 degrees more towards the target than usual, the 5-iron now has 21 degrees of loft. This "new" 5-iron will hit the ball lower and farther than the "old" 5-iron.

The easiest way to change the loft of your club is by altering your ball position. Moving the ball back or forward in your stance, while leaving your hands in the same position, will automatically change the shaft angle and, therefore, the loft of the club.

More advanced players can increase or decrease the loft of the club at impact by modifying their swings. Tiger Woods hits a shot he calls a "Stinger", that most mortals call a "knock down" shot. It is played with the ball back in the stance and a special effort made during the swing to keep the shaft of the club leaning towards the target through impact. The result is a shorter follow through, and a low, penetrating ball flight.

To hit a lower shot, position the ball back in your stance and restrict your follow through to help decrease the loft of the club at impact.

A higher shot can be created by moving the ball up in your stance and making an effort to swing slightly up into the ball. This will add loft to the club and cause a higher ball flight. This technique requires a good lie with cushion under the ball, and the ability to make subtle changes to the location of the bottom of your swing.

To hit a higher shot, position the ball forward in your stance and finish high to help increase the loft of the club at impact.

Challenging Lies

If you are like most golfers, your ball will find its way into some less than desirable spots, over the course of a golf season. The following are tips for handling some common situations, which can test your recovery abilities.

Fairway Bunker

The key to success from fairway bunkers is clean contact. To help ensure good contact, you will need a stable base, established by digging your feet into the sand a couple of inches. Gripping down on the club will compensate for standing below the bottom of the ball.

The swing should be a little shorter than usual, with special attention paid to maintaining your footing and balance. Again, it is imperative that you strike the golf ball first.

For club selection, I suggest you stay with the same club as usual for the short irons, and take an extra club for shots requiring a 7-iron or more. It is always better to hit the ball a little thin, rather than fat, in a fairway bunker. When you hit a ball thin with a short iron it tends to go farther than normal while thin shots with middle and long irons go shorter.

If you have a lip or bank with which to contend, choose a club that will get the ball over the obstacle, even if you hit the ball a little thin. Like all trouble shots, your goal should be to get out of trouble in one shot. If your skill and the shot requirements will allow it, go for the green. If not, take your lumps and make sure you get out of the bunker in one shot.

Fairway bunker shots require a shorter swing to ensure clean contact.

Long Rough

Whoever thought it was a good idea to put long grass bordering the fairway anyway? Many golfers spend a fair bit of time hitting appraoch shots to the green from the rough. Playing shots from long rough requires two main adjustments to your swing.

First, your swing needs to approach the ball on as steep an angle as possible to minimize the amount of grass between the clubface and ball at impact. The more grass between your club and ball at impact, the less control and distance your shots will have.

Secondly, you will need to use plenty of loft, so the ball gets up and out of the long grass quickly. Many golfers make the mistake of using too little loft out of the rough. This causes the ball to launch at a low angle, having to travel through more grass before it gets up into the air. The grass severely slows the ball's speed and a lot of distance is lost.

To help you get the ball up more quickly and to lessen the effects of drag on the clubhead, I suggest you open your clubface a little bit at address. The open clubface will add loft, and let the club glide through the long grass more easily, giving your shot more height and distance.

Another important consideration when playing from the rough, is judging the effects your lie will have on the shot. Some lies in the rough, called flyers, will cause your ball to jump with very little backspin, resulting in a longer shot that rolls further after it lands. Other lies in the rough will cause shots to come out normally, and still others will produce shots that come out with much less speed and travel a much shorter distance than usual. The ability to judge what your lie will do to your shot before hand is crucial to selecting the appropriate shot and club to be played. With experience, you will learn to anticipate the effects of the lie, and make good decisions about your shot. In the short term, play for a flyer when there is trouble behind the green, so if your shot doesn't jump and go farther, your ball will come up a little short. Play for less than average yardage from your club when there is trouble short of the green, so you will clear the potential problems between you and the green, even if the long grass causes you to lose distance.

In a Divot

You have just hit a glorious tee shot down the middle of the fairway, only to find your ball in a huge divot. After a few choice words for the Golf Gods, what do you do?

Playing a shot from a divot is much like the knock-down shot described earlier. Play the ball back in your stance, and strike down quite steeply into the back of the ball, making an abbreviated follow through. You will strike the ball first, and it will come out lower than normal. Factor the lower flight and more roll into your club selection. If it were my choice golfers would always get a preferred lie in their own fairway, but nobody made me King!

Playing in Bad Weather

The two biggest keys for playing in poor weather are: be prepared for the elements and accept the playing conditions and make the best of it. Playing in poor weather will place a premium on controlling the flight of your ball, so the shots described earlier in this chapter will come in very handy.

Bad weather will lead to many more shots ending up off-line. You will need to scramble more often to save pars, making a good short game invaluable.

I like playing in bad weather because I know many golfers get frustrated with the conditions. I know if I stay patient, I will have an advantage. Playing four years of college golf in Seattle, Washington, has prepared me well, for bad weather golf.

Playing in the Wind

Playing in high winds really challenges your ability to control your golf ball. The wind can blow your ball off line, and accentuate the effects of side-spin. Many golfers make the error of trying to hit the ball too hard when they are playing in the wind and they lose control of their shots. I like the phrase, "smooth and easy, whenever it's breezy". Remembering this little rhyme will help keep you under control when the wind is whistling.

The best way to deal with wind is to play your shots close to the ground. Regardless of the wind's direction, if your ball is flying at low altitude, the wind won't affect it much. It takes some skill to be able to control the ball's trajectory, but that's what practice is for!

Into the Wind - Hitting shots into the wind will cause your ball to fly a shorter distance. No news flash there! To lessen the effects of the wind, it is advisable to hit the ball lower. As was described earlier in this chapter, you can hit the ball lower by moving the ball back in your stance and de-lofting your club. It is very important for you not to swing any harder than normal. Making a harder swing will put more backspin on the ball, causing it to climb higher into the air, and land well short of the target.

I like a different approach into the wind. If the distance normally calls for a 7-iron, and you need to hit the ball low to get it to the hole, take a 5 or 6-iron and move your hands down the handle a little bit. Every half inch you grip down will make a club the length of the next club in your bag. For example, if you grip down on your 5-iron one inch, it is now the length of your 7-iron but with less loft. By doing this you don't need to worry about changing your set-up, and you can make your normal swing. Like most trouble shots, you should experiment to learn how the ball will react when you make changes to your set-up and technique.

<u>Cross Winds</u> - You have two options when playing a shot in a cross wind. You can either let your ball be pushed by the wind, or, you can hit an intentional hook or slice so your ball will fight the wind and fly relatively straight.

If you choose to let your ball ride the wind, you will need to figure out how much the wind will push it, and then aim accordingly. It is very similar to putting. You decide how much the shot will "break", and then you aim where the shot needs to start. Shots that ride the wind generally go farther than normal, as they are being pushed along by the wind.

Playing a shot that fights the wind is generally safer, because the shot won't curve as much, and can be aimed more to the middle of the fairway or green. The shot will fly shorter, and does require considerable skill to control the ball flight enough to get predictable results. If you select the shot to curve into the cross wind, and then hit a straight or opposite curve by accident, it will ride the wind and go considerably farther than the distance you had planned.

I recommend you play shots that ride the wind until your ball control is highly developed. If you do, the worst that can happen is you curve the ball into the wind by accident, and it will come up short. Short of the green is generally much better than long.

<u>Down Wind</u> - Your ball will fly farther down wind. The shot will also have less backspin on it, so will roll farther as well. These factors must be considered, when you are selecting your landing spot and club.

Sometimes, when playing a shot down wind, the ball can get knocked down by the wind and will travel a much shorter distance than you would expect. When playing a shot with a strong helping wind, you must make sure the ball gets well up into the air if you are relying on the wind to give your shot additional distance.

<u>Wind Affects the Short Game Too</u> - Chipping and putting in the wind can be challenging as well. When the wind is strong, it can cause short shots to be blown off line, and can even make putts break more or less than the slope would indicate. Make sure you include the effects of the wind when playing short shots on and around the green.

Good putting requires your body to remain very still during the stroke. To keep still in high winds, widen your stance and grip down on your putter, so you can get closer to the ground. On days when the ball is wobbling on the green and looks like the wind may cause it to move, don't ground your putter behind the ball until you are ready to pull the trigger. If the ball moves when your putter is sitting behind the ball it will be a one stroke penalty, but if your putter is hovering above the ground when it moves, there isn't a penalty.

Playing in the Rain

Playing in the rain requires two things: keeping your grips dry at all costs, and if you can, keep yourself dry as well! To do this, you need to be prepared. A big golf umbrella, a good golf bag, a few dry towels, good raingear, and waterproof footwear are all musts. A little trick my old coach showed me, is to carry a package of kleenex on rainy days. A single kleenex will soak up a lot of moisture from your grip when you really need it to be dry.

Rain can cause the golf course to become softer, and the ball to roll more slowly on the greens. Be aware of the changing course conditions, or that the course may already be playing differently than you normally see it.

Playing in Cold Weather

The key to playing well when it's cold is staying warm! Dress in layers. You will have a much larger range of motion if you wear a few thin layers of clothing rather than one or two thick, bulky items. Be sure to wear a hat to cut down on heat loss through your head, and wearing mittens will really help keep your hands warm. Mittens are better than gloves because your fingers can help keep each other warm.

There are hand warmers on the market, which are little packets of powder that get warm when you shake them. They stay warm for a few hours. Having one of these packets in your pocket will do wonders for keeping your hands warm, and your golf game hot!

The golf ball doesn't fly as far in cooler weather so take more club than usual.

Playing in the Heat

Playing golf in high temperatures can be very challenging. It is very important to protect yourself from the harmful effects of the sun by wearing a hat, sunglasses, and plenty of sun screen.

Dehydration is also a major concern for your health and golf game. The symptoms don't show up until it is too late. Drink plenty of water, before and during the round. By the time you feel thirsty, you are already quite dehydrated.

Playing in Competition

Playing in competition is a challenge with which most golfers struggle the first few times. Competition puts the ultimate strain on your ability to remain focused on the shot at hand, and can cause your mind to wander to the final outcome and consequences of your play.

The game of golf doesn't change, it is the importance you place on tournaments that changes your perception. This shift in perceived significance often leads to being distracted and a loss of focus.

All of the skills described in the section on taking your game to the golf course, starting on page 158, apply to playing your best in tournaments. Playing good golf requires you to remain in the now, and pay undivided attention to the shot you are playing. Any concern for the future consequences of a shot, or score, will almost always sabotage your efforts.

I look at tournaments as the ultimate way to test your preparation. If you tend to play worse in tournaments than you do with your friends, the quality of your preparation should be called into question. Specifically, the quality of your mental preparation needs to be improved. The reason a golfer plays worse in tournaments is, he or she hasn't developed the necessary skills to remain focused when the ante is raised. Refer to Chapter Nine for information on improving your mental game. Here are a few more tips on tournament play.

Begin Preparing Well in Advance

As soon as you know the dates of a competition, lay out a plan for how you will prepare. Knowing you have prepared well will give you confidence when the tournament day comes.

As the Tournament Approaches, Your Practice Should Change

Initially, your practice may need to be focussed on improving one or more parts of your game. As the tournament approaches, your practice needs to become more directed towards the playing of the game, and away from your mechanics.

Play a Practice Round

Make a point of getting out to play the course where you will compete. Use this round to survey the course, and put together a game plan for how you will play each hole. If you can, walk the course once without your clubs. Start on the eighteenth green and walk the course backwards to the first tee. This will give you a great perspective on how you should navigate your ball around the course.

Make Sure You Are Well Rested.

Many golfers spend the last few days, before a big event, practicing more than normal. Unfortunately, you can wear yourself down, and show up for the tournament feeling fatigued or burnt out. Include rest and relaxation in your preparation, and show up for the tournament well rested and fresh.

Remind Yourself, "This is why I practice so much".

You will be nervous when it comes time to play. If you're not, it means you don't care enough, and you should consider taking a break from competition. When you are feeling nervous, remind yourself that competing is the reason you work so hard on your game. You shouldn't be scared, you should be excited.

Warm Up, Don't Practice.

Before a tournament round, your time on the practice tee should be spent warming up your body, and readying your mind for competition. Start your warm up on the putting green, getting accustomed to the speed of the greens. Hit a few practice chips, and then move to the range for longer swings. On the range, begin with shorter swings and slowly progress into longer swings with longer clubs. Once your body is warm, spend the rest of your time hitting shots with your pre-shot routine, as you will on the course. Use a few balls to rehearse the most important shots you will face on the course. Finish by hitting a couple of balls with the club you will use on the first tee. You should time your warm up so you finish hitting balls about ten minutes before your tee time, so you don't have a chance to cool off. Find somewhere quiet to gather your thoughts, and then go to the first tee with a few minutes to spare. Over time you will find an ideal length of time for your pre-game warm-up.

One Shot at a Time

It's a cliche, but it's very true. Tournament golf puts the ultimate strain on your ability to remain focused on the task at hand. To play your best during competition, you will need to take each shot as it comes, and do your best with each of them. If you give your complete attention to each shot by gathering information, choosing the right shot, and then going through your pre-shot routine and hitting the shot, you will know at the end of the day you have done your best. If your score isn't to your satisfaction, you will need to adjust your practice approach to get better results the next time. Remembering that your play in tournaments is an assessment of your preparation will help you play your best, and move forward after poor scores. All you can do is try your best on every shot, and then add up your score at the end of the round.

Chapter Summary

- To handle sidehill lies, alter your set-up and aim to allow for the effects of the slope.

- To intentionally curve a ball, aim the club where you want the shot to land and align your body parallel to the direction you want your shot to start.

- To hit high and low shots you must control the loft of the club at impact.

- To play in bad weather, be prepared and accept the poor conditions.

- Playing well in competition requires you to be prepared and have strong mental skills.

Section Three

Learning and Improving

Chapter Twelve
What to Practice

As I discuss in many parts of the book, there are several parts of the game. To play your best you need to spend time practicing each of them. Earlier, I offered my thoughts on each of these departments to help you identify specific things you need to work on to improve your scoring. I firmly believe the bulk of your instruction for technique should come from a qualified instructor, and not from the pages of a book, but I hope my ideas have been helpful.

The main focus of this chapter is helping you decide where to spend your available practice time. I am going to cover two important factors that will help you determine what to practice, and then help you understand the importance of goal setting in the overall effectiveness of your practice time.

The first part of the chapter focuses on how the game breaks down in terms of the percentages of shots used from each different category. The second part will give you advice on how to look at your own game, so you can begin practicing specific weaknesses that are having the greatest effects on your scoring.

My suggestions are all based on the assumption you are looking to lower your scores. Remember, this is the main goal in golf. If you have another agenda in mind, which makes certain parts of the game more important to you than the scores you shoot, the following information will need to be altered to make it applicable to your personal goals.

The Many Parts of Golf

It is widely believed that over 60% of golf shots are played from within 75 yards of the hole. The actual percentage will vary, depending on a golfer's skill level, but the box below shows some general percentages.

Score Breakdown	
Putting	40%
Scoring Game Shots within 75 Yards	15%
Total for Short Game	**55%**
Full Swing Shots	40%
Specialty Shots	5%
Total for Long Game	**45%**

Those numbers are misleading, because the putting data includes short putts from inside 2 feet, which are virtual "gimmes". An average 90-shooter, who has 35 putts, will have tap-ins on at least half of the holes. If those gimmes are thrown out and the remaining 81 shots are used, the putting percentage would drop from about 40% to 33%, and the total short game percentage would drop to about 50%. For this reason, I believe the importance of the scoring game and long game should be considered equal. I realize these numbers are by no means scientifically accurate, but I think they provide a good starting point.

If long game shots and short game shots are of equal importance, a big part of the answer for WHAT you should practice is already obvious.

All parts of the game are important but the skills I rank as most important are:

- The ability to drive the ball in play and far enough to be effective.

- The ability to make a high percentage of putts from ten feet and closer.

- The ability to get your ball inside the ten foot range with your scoring shots, to make one putting more likely.

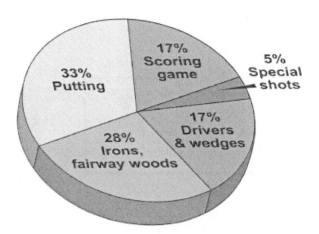

There are many parts of the game that help determine your total score. Understanding them will help you practice effectively.

Another vital component to your golf game's performance is the mental game. The ability to run your brain effectively, will have a huge impact on how well you play on the course. I feel most golfers neglect their mental skills, and this causes the large gap between their practice and playing levels. I covered the mental game in depth in Chapter 9, so you already know its importance. I think 20% is a good estimate for the time you should devote to your mental skills, if you expect to play up to your physical abilities.

You need to divide your remaining practice time equally between your short game, and long game.

Let's break down your practice a little further.

With due consideration given to the "gimme effect" on your short game numbers, it can be estimated that putting accounts for roughly two thirds of your short game strokes. The other third will be comprised of chipping, pitching, sand play and wedge shots. Your short game practice should be broken down accordingly. Forty minutes of every short game practice hour should be spent on your putting. The other twenty minutes should be split evenly between chipping, pitching, sand play and wedge play. Please bear in mind, these numbers are for general use and, as the next section will discuss, you should allocate your own practice time based on a combination of these suggestions, and your personal strengths and weaknesses.

In your long game, roughly 35% of your shots are hit with the clubs you use to tee-off or your wedges. Another 55% are hit with your 9-iron through fairway woods and the remaining 10% are specialty shots requiring control over trajectory or curvature. You should be spending your long game practice time with these percentages in mind.

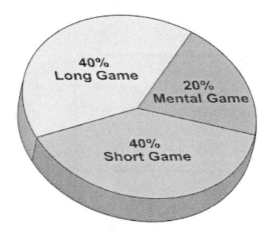

> *Your practice time should
> be divided between
> the different departments
> of the game.*

To put all of these numbers together and solidify your understanding of how your practice time should be spent, let's take a look at an example of a good practice schedule.

The golfer in question has the luxury of spending ten hours a week on his or her game. Doesn't this person have a job? The box below shows how this golfer's practice schedule would look if he or she was really interested in shooting lower scores

Practice Time Breakdown

- 20% on Mental Skills   2 hours
  (visualization, focus and pre-shot routine)

- 40% on Short Game
  - 2.5 hours - putting
  - 0.5 hours - chipping
  - 0.5 hours - pitching
  - 0.5 hours - sand play

- 40% on Long Game
  - 2 hours - driving and wedges
  - 2 hours - 9-iron to fairway woods

Admittedly, there are very few golfers who can spend 10 hours a week practicing their golf, in addition to playing a game or two. Take these percentages and apply them to your own schedule.

Understanding Your Own Game

I hope you now have a clear understanding of how the typical golfer spends his or her shots on the course, and are one step closer to actually practicing the parts of the game as they affect your score.

The other main consideration for allocating practice time is the present state of your game. Recognizing the strengths and weaknesses of your golf game will be very important to the efficiency of your practice time. To improve most quickly, you should spend the majority of your practice time on weaknesses, while spending just enough time on your strengths to maintain their levels.

Most golfers think they have a clear idea of how their game rates in each category. As is the case in most things, our assessment of ourselves is often more flattering than the actual facts! With this in mind, one of the best things you can do for yourself is to begin keeping statistics about your golf game to build an accurate assessment of your strengths and weaknesses.

In Appendix D, I have included the form I use with my students to keep track of their statistics. It is formulated with a few assumptions in mind.

- You need to make putts from four feet and closer to shoot your best scores.

- Your ability to make putts from inside ten feet and avoid three-putting from outside twenty feet will also have a huge impact on your scoring. Even tour pros don't convert many putts from ten feet and beyond, but they rarely three-putt.

- Depending on your skill level, your scoring shots from within 75 yards, need to accomplish one of two things: either get within nine feet of the cup <u>or</u> hit the green every time. Better players hit a higher percentage of their scoring shots to within nine feet resulting in more one putts, while many higher handicappers add several strokes to their score by needing more than one shot from within 75 yards to find the putting surface.

- The ability to hit greens with your irons is important, although, not as important as hitting the fairway with your tee shots. The tee shot sets up the hole, and you rarely hit a full iron shot to within nine feet of the flag.

The form is designed to give you a clear understanding of how the different parts of your game rate. After only a few rounds of keeping your stats, you will see some trends. This information will be very helpful as you plan your practice sessions, and will also be very useful when you are putting together an effective game plan for your play on the course.

Earlier in the chapter I suggested you spend 20% of your practice time on the mental game. It is often difficult to determine whether you need to work on the quality of your technique or your mental game. The way I think you should decide is simple. If your performance in practice is satisfactory to you and would allow you to reach your scoring goals, you really need to work on your mental skills and 20% is probably a conservative estimate for the time you should be spending on them. On the other hand, if your on-course and practice levels are fairly consistent and you aren't playing as well as you would like, your physical skills will need to be upgraded.

If your technique needs improving, deciding what you should work on is best decided with the help of a teaching professional who can offer analysis of each area of your game and help you determine where your efforts should be focused. Correctly diagnosing your problem areas will make your improvement much more likely.

Goal Setting

The final piece of the "what should I be practicing" puzzle will be answered by your goals. You should now have a clear picture of how golf scores are shot with respect to the various parts of the game and in due time you will have some very valuable information by keeping some statistics about your on-course performance. The final step before starting your improvement program is to set some goals for your game and put together a plan for achieving them.

These goals should take into account where your game is at this moment in time, the amount of time you have available for practice, your physical situation and other resources available to you such as practice facilities or competent instruction. It is important that all of these factors be considered so the goals you set are realistic.

There are two kinds of goals: outcome goals, which describe what you want to accomplish, and process goals that focus on what you plan to do to accomplish your outcome goals. Outcome goals can be long term, medium term, and short term. You can set goals for any time frame you like. In the example to follow, I use one year.

Outcome Goals

- One Year (long term) - I will lower my handicap by SIX strokes over the next twelve months.
- Every two months (medium term) - I will lower my handicap by ONE stroke every two months.
- Short term (this week) - I will shoot 82 on Saturday.

Process Goals

- ⚐ Long term - I will practice THREE hours per week on all parts of my game, and take one golf lesson every two weeks.

- ⚐ Every two months - I will evaluate my progress, and refine my practice plan when necessary

- ⚐ Short term - I will allocate practice time to the areas of my game that need special attention based on my strengths and weaknesses, identified through my game stats.

It is very important for your outcome and process goals to be compatible. In this case, it would be foolish to set a goal of shaving six strokes of your handicap, if you didn't have any time to devote to practice.

Once you have set some goals, you need to write them down and post them in a place where you will see them every day. This will give your goals credibility, and will greatly increase the odds of you achieving them. I have included the goal setting form I use with my students in Appendix E, so you can easily put your goals down on paper.

I hope you can see the benefits to making an improvement plan and sticking with it. This will be the road map, which lets you reach your desired destination in the shortest amount of time. You can use your performance on the course to continuously pin point your practice time on the weak areas of your game.

You may discover you need considerable work on one or more phases of your game, or lack the knowledge to work on certain areas. If this is the case, you will benefit by getting instruction from a PGA Teaching Professional in your area. Working with a good teacher, will streamline your improvement efforts, and let you reach your goals more quickly.

Chapter Summary

- Your final score is determined by totalling the number of many different kinds of shots.

- Depending on the golfer, roughly half of his or her shots are short game and half are full swing.

- Keeping stats about your game will help you pin-point practice time on the weakest parts of your game.

- Long and short-term goals will provide a road map for your improvement journey.

Chapter Thirteen
How to Practice

I have just spent the last chapter detailing how you should be spending more of your practice time on all parts of the game, rather than just the full swing. I really hope you use this approach to your practice, because I know if you do, it will really help your game. This chapter will focus more on how to practice, and I will once again ask you to be different than most golfers.

Be Specific About What You Intend to Practice

How to practice for steady and permanent improvement is the million-dollar question. The answer is an easy one. Decide what skill you need to improve, and then work on it with complete focus. When I was on tour, my coach used to say, "do what you're doin' while you're doin' it". That was his way of telling me to remain focused on the task at hand.

In addition to working on your technique in the many phases of the game, you must also work on just playing golf.

One of the biggest obstacles to your improvement is the need for different mindsets when learning and playing the game. You need to be a bit of a perfectionist to learn the mechanics of the swing and other parts of the game, willing to put in the time to engrain the proper habits. When playing, you need to be more carefree and simply try to hit your ball to the target, without any thoughts about mechanics.

Most golfers wind up being stuck between these two mindsets when they practice and play. While working on swing mechanics, golfers remain overly concerned with the quality of their shots and when playing golf, they remain worried about their swing mechanics. This cycle causes the golfer to engrain the same old swing habits during practice, and to be distracted by mechanical thoughts when trying to play golf. Improvement is hampered.

For maximum efficiency with your practice, you must be decisive about the kind of practice in which you intend to engage. There is practice to strengthen your techniques in the different compartments of the game, and there is what I call GOLF practice. Golf practice involves making your practice as close to game-like conditions as possible to prepare you for the golf course. It is in this last kind of practice where you will work on getting out of your own way and letting your technique perform to its potential.

> When trying to improve your technique, your entire focus must be on the motion you are trying to turn into a habit.
>
> When practicing GOLF, your entire focus must be on getting your ball to go to the TARGET.

To make improvements to your swing, putting stroke, or mental skills you need to isolate the particular skill that needs attention, and focus entirely on the desired changes. If it is a change to your backswing, for example, you will need to do countless repetitions of the new and improved movement with absolutely no concern for where the ball is going. Body awareness, not shot quality, should be used to critique your backswing. It is entirely possible to make a fundamentally sound backswing and still hit a poor shot.

If your set-up, backswing and finish position are sound, and it is better accuracy you desire, you must relinquish any thoughts of your backswing mechanics, and focus entirely on the targeting skill you want to improve.

In a perfect world, you would spend time perfecting your set-up position, making a good backswing repeatable, and would then solidify your forward swing so you could finish your swing in balance. When these parts of the swing were automatic, you would turn your attention to learning the targeting skills of solid contact, clubface control and swing path.

In this ideal scenario, the ball would be introduced when you were able to make mechanically sound and balanced golf swings in your sleep and were ready to work on shot quality. The golf ball is the ultimate targeting coach.

The problem most golfers face is that the introduction of the golf ball tends to pull their attention away from whichever mechanical improvement they are trying to implement. This distraction usually results in the golfer's inability to stick with the new mechanics long enough to create new habits because concern over ball flight causes him or her to focus on targeting before the swing is ready to handle it.

When you are ready to begin refining targeting skills, you should work on the ability to control the clubface first. I recommend this, because the tendency to flip or scoop with the hands through impact leads to contact and path problems. When you learn to use the clubface correctly, you can then develop contact and path skills quite easily.

The improvement of targeting skills will be dependant on the quality of your set-up and backswing, but cannot be worked on while thinking about those parts of your technique. Practicing your targeting skills requires complete attention to the specific skill to be improved, whether it be solid contact, clubface control, or swing path.

It is not productive to work on your swing path until you are confident in your ability to control the clubface and, therefore, the curvature on your golf ball. Many golfers and teaching professionals focus on the outside-to-in swing path as the cause of a slice. I believe golfers learn the outside-to-in swing path BECAUSE they slice. When a golfer hits ball after ball that slices, he or she would have to be insane to continue swinging towards the target. After only a few slices, the golfer quickly learns to start swinging the club from outside-to-in to help counteract the anticipated slice on the golf shot. Unfortunately, this is like gas on a fire, because the body motions required to swing the club this way generally cause an even bigger slice.

It is for the above reasons, I always work to give my students control over the clubface first. I believe the clubface rules the golf swing. Until you can hit golf shots that have a consistent and manageable curve to them, you will struggle to play consistent golf. Once you can learn to control the ball's behavior in flight, the game becomes easy, because all you need to do is swing the club towards the target. You have been doing that in other sports and activities your whole life. Even if you haven't played any other sports, you still have the ability to swing your hands in the direction of a target.

Every practice session should include at least a little bit of golf practice. With the last few balls, hit each one with a different target in mind, and a different club in hand.

Practicing golf is the phase, which combines all your skills, and prepares you for the golf course. Your challenge is to make every shot struck during golf practice as important as the most critical shot you will face in competition.

Effective Practice

Some keys to effective practice are:

- Set goals based on where your game is, and where you would like it to be. Advice from a pro is often helpful.

- Decide what you need to work on to reach your goals - mechanics or golf. Again, expert advice will ensure an accurate assessment, and will help you avoid wasted time spent working on the wrong things.

- Set specific goals for each practice session with your ultimate goal in mind.

- Use practice suggestions in this chapter to improve habits in weak areas of your game, and further strengthen your whole game.

- Assess progress regularly, and adjust practice schedule and focus as necessary.

Let's take a look at the best ways to improve specific parts of your game. Later in this chapter, I will give you advice on how to tie all the skills together during golf practice, so you can take your game from the range to the golf course.

Improving Your Technique

Ultimately, what you are looking at when you decide to improve your swing, or some other part of your golf game, is the creation of new habits. In golf, habits are movements or thought processes that can be performed without the need for conscious thought.

Most people respond to pressure by falling back on old habits. All you have to do is make sure those old habits are good habits!

Making changes to habits can be accomplished in a couple of ways. The process chosen must be completed, so the new skill can be performed while you are focused on the target.

It is very common for golfers who begin playing as children to learn the golf swing more quickly than their adult counterparts. Children learn the easy way, while adults tend to go about it differently. When kids start playing golf, they are just having fun, and haven't been brainwashed into thinking golf is difficult, or that the golf swing requires a lot of hard work to learn. Children learn most things by imitating. It is well documented, that the reason Phil Mickelson swings left-handed, is that his father swung right-handed and Phil simply learned how to swing by using his dad's swing as a mirror image. The result is the loose and natural looking swing we get to watch on TV many Sunday afternoons.

The Easy Way

The process of imitation is every bit as effective as the other way of learning I will outline later in this chapter. Unfortunately, most adults who are learning the game, are unable to buy into its simplicity, and feel the need to try the other approach. The ultimate problem, as we will see later, is most adults don't really use the other approach either!

Here is the simple approach for all of you who might want to give it a try. This does work. It is important that you follow the steps in order, and don't move on until the successful completion of each step.

Step One - Decide on your own, or get professional advice, on the swing improvements that need to be made.

Step Two - Pick an appropriate model whose swing exhibits the desired motion, and who you feel you can copy. Pick a model who is built like you, and possesses similar physical capabilities.

Once you have selected your model, spend considerable time imagining his or her swing. Visualize your model, correctly performing the desired movement, until you can "see" his or her swing in your head over and over without any fluctuation in the quality of the images. You will find, at first, the vision of the swing is choppy and hard to see from start to finish. With some practice you will be able to watch your model's swing without interruption or degradation of picture quality. Once you can watch your model's swing repeatedly, with total clarity, you are ready to move on to Step Three.

Step Three - Imagine the swing motion of your model, but now replace his or her face with yours. Repeat the same procedures as in Step One until you can visualize yourself perform the desired swing repeatedly without interruption. When you can watch yourself perform the desired swing without fluctuation, you are ready to move on to Step Four.

Step Four - You become your model. You actually use a golf club and perform the skill you have been watching yourself perform in Step Three. You can now feel the swings you have been watching. Allow yourself to make swings using pictures and not verbal commands. Enjoy the feeling of the new and competent motion you are making.

Step Five - You validate your newly learned skill, and allow yourself to move on to learning a new skill or simply playing the game.

You may remember using this technique when you were learning other things as a kid. I remember being on the putting green at dusk when I was 13 or 14, imagining I was Jack

Nicklaus putting to win the 1978 U.S. Open. Other times, I was Bobby Orr "flying" down the left wing, and letting that "wicked" shot go, that the goalie never would have stopped! Eventually, it was me putting to win the U.S. Open to beat Jack in a playoff. Back then it was easy to learn new things. I didn't have any expectations or any concerns about failure because I was just having fun. Many adults have concerns about what others will think about them, when they start golf. Others have high expectations because they have been successful in other sports or endeavors. One thing's for sure, most adults try to over control the learning process. If you can regain your ability to be a kid and use the steps I have just outlined, you will learn to play golf very quickly, and with relatively little effort. If you feel the need to work at something before earning the right to play well, keep reading.

The Adult Way (The Hard Way)

<u>Step One</u> - Decide on your own, or get professional advice on the swing improvements that need to be made.

<u>Step Two</u> - Ensure you can perform desired skill perfectly every time with help of mirror or educated observer.

<u>Step Three</u> - When feel for desired motion has been developed, continue repetition of desired skill with complete focus on that skill alone. It is preferable that you perform the repetitions without golf balls. If you absolutely have to hit golf balls, it is vital that you focus entirely on the successful completion of your desired skill. Judgment of success or failure should hinge on the quality of the desired motion, and not the resulting ball flight. Any concern for ball flight will sabotage your efforts, and seriously delay or stop the acquisition of the new skill. This is the prime reason most golfers struggle to improve their swings. They don't perform enough high quality repetitions of a skill to make it a habit.

When the movement is new, you will be tense and disjointed in your movements and your golf shots will be predictably substandard. This is the classic, one step backwards for two steps forward scenario. After completing sufficient repetitions to learn the new swing habit, you can then move on to the final step.

<u>Step Four</u> - You validate your newly learned skill, and allow yourself to move on to learning a new skill or simply playing the game. This is a very difficult step for many adult golfers because they are so accustomed to fixing their swings repeatedly. It is vital that you take the time to congratulate yourself and acknowledge the new skill so you can keep improving.

You are probably saying to yourself, "I don't have the time to do all that". I would like to challenge you on that idea.

Remember, you don't need golf balls to learn a fundamentally sound golf swing. As a result, you can learn a new backswing or set-up change in the comfort of your own home or office. To perform a backswing or putting stroke, even in slow motion, takes no more than a couple of seconds. To perform several with total focus would not take more than ten or fifteen minutes a day. If you really want to improve, you can certainly find ten or fifteen minutes a day to practice your golf swing.

With these facts in mind, it is my opinion that you will improve most quickly if you work on your technique at home, or without a golf ball. Use the golf ball to work only on your targeting skills. I haven't met many golfers who can hit a golf ball successfully while completely focusing on a certain swing motion in their backswing. That includes the author of this book!

If you attempt to work on both habit formation and targeting at the same time, you will never truly learn the new habit. In this all too familiar pattern, new habits are never learned and your swing remains the same. A golfer in this cycle can never leave swing mechanics behind and is never able to move on to just playing golf. If you are a golfer who is always trying new things or find it hard to quiet your mind of mechanical thoughts when playing on the course, you need to change your approach to your golf swing. Get some sound advice on necessary swing improvements, go through the required steps to solidify your technique, and move on to playing *golf* and not *golf swing*.

Developing Targeting Skills

The best methods for developing your targeting skills are included in the chapters pertaining to each part of the game. In general, you will learn most quickly by starting out with smaller swings and building to larger swings, or longer shots, when your results warrant it. I'm a big believer that if you can't hit a solidly struck, straight shot with a half swing, you aren't ready to make a full swing. The same could be said for putting or chipping. If you can't make a two-foot putt every time, you aren't ready to make longer putting strokes.

When you are ready to work on your targeting skills, it is imperitive that your set-up position is the same for every practice ball. For the golf ball to give you usable feedback, you must be aligned correctly, and use the same start position every time. If your alignment or other pre-shot fundamentals change all the time, you are asking your brain to constantly make adjustments to your swing to react to an ever changing orientation to the ball and target.

Learning targeting skills relies on good swing mechanics. Spend time to ensure your swing motion is sound before you try to learn targeting skills with your full swing.

> **tip time!**
>
> When practicing targeting skills, use a "work station" to ensure you set-up position is the same every time.

Practicing Golf - Taking Your Game to the Course

I use the term "practicing golf" to describe practice designed to prepare you for the golf course. This is the time when the mental game skills you have been developing at home can be used to set the stage for your best possible performance. Bear in mind, all you can hope to accomplish with your "golf" practice, is to make it possible for you to play up to your capabilities on the course. If your golf swing or putting stroke has technical flaws, a sound mental game will not mask them. A sound mental game only serves to eliminate mental interference, so all of your talent can be utilized, whatever your talent level may be.

One of the biggest reasons golfers have trouble taking their game from the practice tee to the course is their failure to spend enough time practicing golf. Most average golfers spend their time on the practice tee, rapid firing ball after ball. They are lulled into a sense of comfort by the fact that no one is watching where their balls are going and if they hit a poor shot they still have 70 balls left in their bucket. After hitting a number of 5-irons in a row, they get a bit of a rhythm going and hit a few good ones. These golfers leave the range feeling good about their games, only to discover they have lost the magic when they show up at the course the next day.

On the golf course, you are faced with several challenges. There are hazards bordering many of the holes, you only have one ball, and everyone in your group knows where you are aiming. If you haven't prepared for this, you will probably struggle to perform.

To effectively take your game to the course, you must learn to hit golf shots thinking only about the target. Golf is a target game, and is played best without mechanical thoughts.

The overload of stimuli causes you to lose your focus on the shot at hand. You can become distracted by images of poor shots, expected judgments by playing partners, or thoughts about your score. These distractions will always affect your play if you don't develop a strategy to deal with them, and it all begins with how you practice.

The key to performing up to your skill level on the course, is to make your practice seem as real as possible. The best way to take your game from the range to the course is to bring the course to the range. This is accomplished by being very specific about the targets you select during practice, going through your pre-shot routine before every shot, and switching clubs and targets after each ball. I don't know about you, but I rarely hit fifteen 6-irons in a row on the course!

The pre-shot routine mentioned earlier is a vital tool for playing your best golf. A good routine will utilize many skills. These skills must be developed, and then combined into a 40 – 50 second routine you use to hit each golf shot.

The following points are a reminder of the steps required for a good pre-shot routine:

- Gather information about how the ball is sitting, select an appropriate and precise target, calculate your distance to that target, and consider all factors, which will affect your ball's flight and roll on its way to the target.

- Formulate this information into a plan for the shot, complete with images of the ball flight needed to get the ball to the target. The shot selection must be consistent with your current playing ability.

- Choose the club and technique required for the shot that has been selected.

- Visualize the desired shot.

- Rehearse the swing required for the shot.

- Complete the steps of your routine leading you to a good set-up position without any deviation in your focus on the desired outcome.

- Execute the shot while maintaining focus on your target.

The level of your play will be determined by your physical talents in each part of the game and the quality of your mental skills that allows them to be used. A good pre-shot routine goes a long way to eliminating mental interference that blocks your physical skills from performing.

The Anatomy of a Good Practice Session

To make your practice time most productive, you should always have clear goals in mind before you arrive at the practice tee, or short game area. Having a plan for how your session will go is necessary, so you can avoid falling into the trap of bouncing from one topic to another. It is also important for you to limit the length of your sessions. You should never practice for longer than 45 minutes without taking a break, and it is always better to schedule several short sessions rather than one practice marathon.

As your technique gets better, or if you have more practice time available to you, the amount of time spent on golf practice should be increased considerably. Remember, practicing golf is what will prepare you for the course.

There is plenty of room for customizing your practice sessions to your specific needs, but, like your game plan for the course, making a plan in advance will let you focus on the execution of the plan, rather than having to make decisions on the fly about what you should practice.

A Typical 60-Minute Practice Session

Warm Up (5 – 10 minutes)
Begin with stretching, move into small swings, and then progress to longer and faster swings when your body is ready to handle it.

Skill Building (20 – 45 minutes)
This time should be spent working on a specific pre-determined area of your game, such as your backswing or speed control in your putting game.

Short Break (5 minutes)
Take some time to have a drink of water or talk with a friend.

Practice Golf (the remainder of the session)
Spend at least the last 5 minutes, preferably longer, on practicing golf. Hit one shot at a time to a new target each time and use your routine on every shot. Ending your session this way will get you back to target mode and ready for your next game.

Chapter Summary

- Be specific about what you intend to work on during every practice session.

- When working on swing mechanics, worry only about the motion you are trying to perform.

- When working on targeting, worry only about the ball flight you are getting.

- Always use a practice station to ensure your good pre-shot fundamentals are maintained.

- End every practice session by practicing GOLF.

Chapter Fourteen
The Role of a Teaching Professional

As you can tell by the last couple of chapters, making improvements to your golf game involves some important decisions and a lot of practice. A qualified Teaching Professional can help shorten the process significantly with expert advice about every step required.

The most important thing a PGA Teaching Professional can give you is personalized attention. I have stated several times, the difficulties with trying to learn a golf swing or a putting stroke from a book. I hope this book helps put your game into perspective and has offered guidance on how to maximize the efficiency of your practice sessions. It should also have introduced you to some new concepts on the mental game and course management. I hope you will take my advice and enlist the services of a qualified teaching professional for help with your game, so the instruction you are getting is 100% appropriate for you.

Help With Your Goal Setting

A PGA Professional will be able to give you an assessment of your current skills, and together with your available time for practice, help you set realistic goals for your game. If you are eighty years old and four feet tall you will never hit the ball as far as Tiger Woods. On the flip side, if you have lots of time to practice, and are in good shape, wanting to shave one stroke off your handicap this golf season is probably selling yourself short. Your teacher will make sure your goals fit your situation and help you avoid frustration and disappointment.

> *If you really want to improve, coaching from a PGA Teaching Professional in your area is the best way to make it happen.*

An Expert Pair of Eyes

As you know, you can't see yourself swing. A teaching professional will be able to watch you and quickly diagnose the problems to be fixed. A good teacher thoroughly understands the cause and effect relationships in golf swings, and will focus your practice efforts on the root cause of the poor shots. Even when you take video of yourself and look at it in slow motion, you may not have the knowledge necessary to correctly identify the most important faults needing to be fixed.

After the problem has been identified, your teacher will provide you with valuable feedback on the quality of your practice repetitions. If you are like most golfers, what you feel you're doing and are actually doing is quite different. An accurate assessment of your current movements will let you link what you feel with what you're really doing. Working until you correctly execute the new motion, and understanding how it needs to feel, will ensure you are engraining the correct mechanics in subsequent practice sessions.

Get Specific Advice on How to Practice

Once the problems have been diagnosed, your teacher will prescribe exactly what you should be focusing on during you practice sessions. As mentioned in Chapter Thirteen, how you spend your practice time will have a huge effect on your improvement. Expert advice on how to spend your practice time will make it most efficient.

Keep You on Track

A teaching professional will keep you on the right track towards your goals. It is very easy to become side-tracked, and begin working on something new before you should. Many golfers make the mistake of moving on to a new part of the swing long before they have completely learned the previous step. Your golf game is like a house, before you can add another floor to your home, the foundation and floor below must be solid. It is the job of your teacher to ensure you stay with each step until you are ready to build on it.

Benefit From Their Experience

Golf professionals have seen and done almost everything. You may view them as experts, but remember, they were at your level at some time during their development as golfers. They have tried almost everything, and been in many different situations, so they are in a position to really help you by conveying their experiences. By listening to your teacher's stories about what they have been through, you may be able to avoid making the same mistakes and will reach your goals quicker as a result.

Experienced PGA Teaching Professionals will provide you with expert instruction on what and how to practice. They will help you prioritize your needs, and tell you which areas of your game need improving, to reach your goals. They can then advise you on the changes in your technique needed for improvement and ensure the information you are using is applicable to you. If you really want to improve, a qualified instructor will help you reach your goals quickly, and with the least amount of frustration.

Chapter Summary

If you really want to improve, spend some time with a qualified PGA Teaching Professional in your area. You'll be glad you did.

Conclusion

Golf is the greatest game on earth. In recent years, technology has made golf clubs more forgiving than ever before, and improved the conditions of golf courses dramatically. One would assume, with these advancements, the golfing population would be shooting progressively lower scores. They aren't.

The reason they aren't is that almost all golfers are still approaching the game the same way they always have. They are still suffering from the effects of using the wrong information, and they continue to use their practice time ineffectively.

I hope this book has helped you see the light, and will help start you on the way to playing the golf of your dreams.

Thank you for letting me be a part of your golf game, and good luck.

Glossary

Anchoring - The act of depositing an event in your memory banks with emotion. This process makes it far more likely that you will remember the event in the future.

Address - Your set-up position

Break - The amount of curve you must allow for a putt on a green that isn't flat.

Chunk - A type of shot casued by hitting behind the ball, as in a "chunked" shot.

Closed - Clubface pointed to the left of your ultimate target at address or impact. (right-handed golfer)

Closed Stance - Player sets up with some or all of his or her body aligned to the right of the target. (right-handed golfer)

Custom Fit - The process of having your golf clubs sized for you based on your body type and swing motion.

Draw - A golf shot that curves gently from right-to-left for a right-handed golfer.

Driver - The 1-wood. All other woods are called "fairway woods".

Fat Shot - A shot caused by the club hitting the ground before the ball. Sometimes referred to as, "hitting the big ball first".

Forward Press - Targetward shift of the hands just before starting the swing or putting stroke.

Fade - A shot that has a gentle curve from left-to-right for a right-handed golfer.

Gap Wedge - A wedge with roughly 52 degrees of loft. Called a gap wedge because it fits in the "gap" between the pitching wedge and sand wedge.

Golf - A target sport that is played by sending a white ball towards a hole in the ground. Not to be confused with "golf swing", which is a motion used to play golf.

Golf Swing - An athletic motion that is learned and then used to play golf.

Hook - Type of shot, for a right-handed golfer, that curves dramatically to the left, usually finishing well left of the target. A hook is normally considered to be a non-desirable shot.

Inside - The area on the golfer's side of the ball and target line. Everything beyond the ball and target line is referred to as "outside". These terms are most often used when describing the swing path with such phrases as outside-to-inside.

Leading Edge - The forward most part of the club. The bottom edge of the clubface.

Lie - How your ball is sitting

Lie Angle - The angle at which the shaft comes out of the head of your golf club.

Loft - The built-in angle of the clubface, responsible for getting the ball in the air.

Open - Clubface looking to the right of your ultimate target at address or impact. (right-handed golfer)

Open Stance - Player sets up with some or all of his or her body aligned to the left of the target. (right-handed golfer)

Over the Top - A term that describes the situation when the golf club swings out and over the ideal swing plane at the start of the forward swing. This results in an outside-to-in swing path through impact.

Path - The direction of the swing as it passes through the ball.

Preparation - The set-up and backswing. The part of the swing when you are preparing to swing the club towards the target.

Scoring Lines - The grooves on the face of a golf club.

Thin Shot - A low shot caused by striking the ball close to the blunt, leading edge of the club rather than the centre of the lofted face of the club.

Skull - Similar to a "thin shot" only lower on the club. Causes a very low shot. Sometimes spelled "scull" as in the glancing motion of an oar that makes improper contact with the water.

Slice - A shot that curves dramatically to the right for a right-handed golfer, most often more that the player desires. A slice is the most common shot among amateur golfers.

Square - Clubface looking directly at the hole at address/impact.

Square Stance - A stance where your feet, knees, hips and shoulders are all parallel to your intended target line

Sweet Spot - Perfect point on the clubface with which to strike the ball. Usually positioned very near the centre of the clubface.

Swing Plane - Angle at which the club shaft travels around the body during a swing.

Target Line - A straight line that joins the golf ball and the target.

Targeting Skills - The skills of solid contact, clubface control and swing path.

appendices

The following pages include many of the forms I use with my students to help them focus their practice sessions, and get the most out of their games.

Appendix A - Total Game Checklist

This is a form that will let you systematically work on all the skills needed to play your best golf. It is very comprehensive, so please don't be alarmed by the quantity of skills needed to play good golf. It is merely a tool to ensure you don't overlook any of the important areas of the game.

Appendix B - Game Statistics Form

This form will make it easy for you to keep track of how you spend your strokes on the course. These stats will help you allocate your practice time effectively, and let you make smarter decisions on the course.

Appendix C - Putting Asssessment Form

A great way to check your putting skills and chronicle your improvement over time.

Appendix D - Scoring Game Assessment Form

A great test for your scoring shots to make practice more productive and fun.

Appendix E - Goal Setting Forms

A form that will make it easy for you to put your goals down on paper. As you know, writing your goals down is an important part of reaching your potential.

Appendix A - Total Game Checklist

I designed this checklist to help you take an inventory of your game. It emphasizes the concepts and skills I feel are important for you to reach your golfing potential. As you read the list, determine if improvements are required in each category for you to reach your goals. If you are satisfied with your present level, put a check mark in the box provided.

A Foundation of Knowledge

Three Vital Concepts - Page 5
- ☐ I understand the concepts governing solid contact
- ☐ I understand the concepts governing clubface control
- ☐ I understand the concepts governing the proper swing path

Ball Flight Laws - Page 17
- ☐ I understand what the club does to cause the nine different ball flights

Equipment - Page 29
- ☐ My body is in good condition
- ☐ My golf clubs are perfectly suited to me and my skill level.
- ☐ My eyes are giving me accurate information.

The Full Swing

The Set Up - Preparation - Page 47
- ☐ I have a good Grip
- ☐ I have good Posture
- ☐ I understand the concpets governing Ball Placement
- ☐ I know how to aim the clubface and align my body correctly

The Backswing - More Preparation - Page 53
- ☐ My swing is in good shape at Checkpoint 1
- ☐ My swing is in good shape at Checkpoint 2
- ☐ My swing is in good shape at the end of my backswing

The Forward Swing - Targeting Skills - Page 60
- ☐ Solid Contact - I am good at locating the bottom of my swing correctly
- ☐ Clubface Control - I am good at timing the rotation of the clubface
- ☐ Proper Path - I can swing the club from inside the target line, out to the target
- ☐ My swing always ends in a balanced finish

Putting

Proper Equipment - Page 36
- ☐ My putter is the correct length for me.
- ☐ I find it easy to aim my putter.
- ☐ I like the look and feel of my putter.

Your Set-Up - Page 70
- ☐ I have a good putting grip
- ☐ I have good posture and correct eye position over the target line
- ☐ I always have correct ball position
- ☐ I am good at aiming my putterface and aligning my body

The Stroke - Page 72
- ☐ I make solid contact
- ☐ I have good directional control (putter aim and path)
- ☐ I have good distance control

Green Reading - Page 76
- ☐ I always consider speed and break factors in that order
- ☐ I am good at choosing the correct line for my putts

The Scoring Game

Chipping - Page 88
- ☐ I make consistently solid contact
- ☐ I have learned good distance control
- ☐ I have learned to control the roll on my chips with club selection

Pitching - Page 89
- ☐ I make consistently solid contact
- ☐ I have learned distance control by varying my swing length
- ☐ I have learned to control the roll on my pitches with trajectory

Wedge Play - Page 90
- ☐ I make consistently solid contact
- ☐ I have learned distance control with the "3 Swing System"
- ☐ I have learned to control the roll with good shot selection

Sand Play - Page 92
- ☐ I make consistent contact
- ☐ I have learned distance control by varying my swing length
- ☐ I have learned to control roll with loft and spin

The Mental Game

Running Your Brain - Page 105
- ☐ I am good at focusing and concentrating
- ☐ I am good at staying relaxed
- ☐ I am able to clearly visualize my swing or the shots I am playing
- ☐ I am good at maintaining my emotional stability
- ☐ I ALWAYS use my Pre-Shot Routine during play and practice
- ☐ I use a consitent Post-Shot Routine to control what my brain is learning

Course Management

Know Your Own Game - Page 117
- ☐ I chart my game for a firm grasp on my strengths and weaknesses.
- ☐ I know how far my clubs hit the ball through the air.

Have a Game Plan - Page 118
- ☐ I set a personal par for each hole?
- ☐ I plan my strategy for every hole I play based on my personal par.
- ☐ I only try shots within my abilities – I play my own game.
- ☐ I use my pre-shot routine on every shot.

Special Skills

Side Hill Lies - Page 127
- ☐ I know how to handel a balls above and below my feet
- ☐ I know how to handle uphill and downhill lies

Shot Making - Page 129
- ☐ I can intentionally make my shots curve from right to left
- ☐ I can intentionally make my shots curve from left to right
- ☐ I can hit high and low shots

Playing in Bad Weather - Page 134
- ☐ I am good at playing in rain and wind
- ☐ I am good at playing in cold or heat

Playing in Competition - Page 137
- ☐ I am always well prepared
- ☐ I know haow to play effective practice rounds
- ☐ I use a good warm-up session before every tournament round
- ☐ I perform well under pressure

Practice Skills

Goal Setting - Page 148
- ☐   I set outcome and process goals for each season
- ☐   I set long, medium, and short term goals.
- ☐   I have goals for each practice session.

What to Practice - Page 143
- ☐   I understand how the game breaks down and practice accordingly.
- ☐   I spend plenty of time working on my weaknesses to make them strengths.

How to Practice - Page 151
- ☐   I am very specific about what I practice.
- ☐   When working on my GOLF SWING, I only evaluate the quality of my swing motion.
- ☐   When working on GOLF, I only evaluate the quality of my shot.

When you have check marks in every box, you're ready for the tour!

Appendix B - Putting Assessment

Lag Putting - 10 putts

Putt two balls from 20 ' .... # of 3-Putts _____

Putt three balls from 30 ' .... # of 3-Putts _____

Putt three balls from 40 ' .... # of 3-Putts _____

Putt two balls from 50 ' .... # of 3-Putts _____

Total # of 3-Putts _____

Makeable Putts - 20 putts

Putt ten balls from 3 - 4 feet .... # made _____

Putt ten balls from 4 - 9 feet .... # made _____

Total # of Putts Made _____

Alternate putting uphill, downhill, and sidehill putts during
both parts of the assessment.

Appendix C - Scoring Game Test

Chip Shots - 10 shots
(from edge of green)

	from 30'	from 50'
Holed out	__ / 5	__ / 5
0 – 3 feet	__ / 5	__ / 5
3 - 6 feet	__ / 5	__ / 5
6 - 9 feet	__ / 5	__ / 5
over 9 feet	__ / 5	__ / 5

Pitch Shots - 10 shots
(10 yds. from edge of green, 30 yds. from hole)

Holed out	__ / 10
0 – 5 feet	__ / 10
5 – 10 feet	__ / 10
10 – 15 feet	__ / 10
over 15 feet	__ / 10

Wedge Shot - 10 shots
(2 shots from 20, 40, 60, 80 and 100 yards)

Hit target	__ / 10
Landed within 0 – 10 feet	__ / 10
Landed within 10 - 20 feet	__ / 10
Landed within 20 - 30 feet	__ / 10
Landed further than 30 feet	__ / 10

Bunker Shots - 10 shots

Holed out	__ / 10
0 – 4 feet	__ / 10
4 – 10 feet	__ / 10
10 – 15 feet	__ / 10
over 15 feet	__ / 10

Date Completed : _____

Appendix D - Game Statistics Form

Record number of successes over total number of attempts.

Date : _____

Putting

Putts made inside 4'	__ / __
Putts made 4 to 10'	__ / __
Putts made 10 to 30'	__ / __
3 putts from 10' +	__ / __

Chipping

Chip-ins	__ / __
Shots to within 4 '	__ / __

Sand Saves

Shots to within 10 '	__ / __

Pitching

Shots to within 4 '	__ / __
Shots to within 4 - 10 '	__ / __
Shots to 10 ' or more	__ / __

Greens Hit (full shots)

8, 9 PW, SW	__ / __
5, 6, 7 irons	__ / __
2, 3, 4 irons	__ / __
Fairway Woods	__ / __

Tee Shots

Hit Fairway	__ / __
In Rough	__ / __
Out of Play	__ / __

Specialty Shots

Successful	__ / __

Mental Game

Pre-Shot Routine	__ / __

Golf Score: _____

Appendix E - Goal Setting Forms

Outcome Goals

Long Range

Completion Date   _____

Goal Description   _____
    _____
    _____

Medium Range

Completion Date   _____

Goal Description   _____
    _____
    _____

Short Range

Completion Date   _____

Goal Description   _____
    _____
    _____

You may need to use multiple forms if you have several goals.

Process or Action Goals

Long Range

Plan of Action

_____

_____

_____

_____

Medium Range

Plan of Action

_____

_____

_____

_____

Short Range

Plan of Action

_____

_____

_____

_____

You may need to use multiple forms if you have several goals.

Potential Obstacles and Strategies

Obstacle

Description: _____

_____

Strategy to overcome: _____

_____

_____

_____

Obstacle

Description: _____

_____

Strategy to Overcome: _____

_____

_____

_____

You may need to use multiple forms if you have several goals.

Notes

Notes

Notes

ISBN 1553957784